Mythical Flower Stories

By

Marilyn Reid

Marilyn Reid
28 Glen Grove
Newtonmore
Scotland, U.K.

Phone: 01540 570036

E.Mail: Marilyn @MarilynReid.com

ISBN 978-1-84753-521-4

D0308489

Dedication

To My Daughter... Hayley

CONTENTS

21,142 words

CONTENTS

Flowers – by Thomas P. Moses (1808 – 1881)

'Tis early dawn - and all around
Bright dewy flowers I view,
Uprising from the fertile ground,
Of every form and hue.
The waving trees in silken sheen
Unfold their blossoms gay;
And on each festooned bough are seen
Young minstrel birds at play.

The vale, and hill, and balmy grove,
With dewy gems are bright;
In mountain wilds, where're we rove,
Beauty attracts our sight;
The carolling of happy birds
More joyous makes the scene;
And pleasant 'tis to view the herds
Trip round the velvet green.

'Tis morn - I trace the rosy aisles
Of yonder garden rare;
Each swelling bud seems fraught with smiles
That thinking hearts may share.
The tall carnation pink is by,
With breath of incense sweet,
Unfolding splendours to each eye
That will its beauties greet.

I sit me by the tulip mound
Where Fancy sheds her light;
Here gems of every tint abound,
Most charming to the sight.
The lily of the valley, too,
And the forget-me-not,
Come forth as stars of light anew
To gild the garden spot.
The damask rose and myrtle flowers,
Narcissus and sweet pea,
With lustre shine in garden bowers,

As stars shine on the sea.
Nature in loveliness appears,
To gladden every mind;
She may dispel our sighs and tears;
True joys in her we find.

'Tis noon - I rest by purling stream,
Where grows the ivy vine;
Here oft I've strayed in youthful dream,
Plucking the columbine.
O, I will sing of flowers - a theme
For loftiest pen to dwell;
How faint must weaker efforts seem
Their charms divine to tell!

Where is the hand would crush a flower,
Unheedful of its worth?
He who outpours the genial shower
Is author of its birth.
O, bring me flowers when the last,
Last pulse has told its tale;
They'll cheer the scene amid the blast
That turns the features pale.

'Tis early dawn - and all around
Bright dewy flowers I view,
Uprising from the fertile ground,
Of every form and hue.
The waving trees in silken sheen
Unfold their blossoms gay;
And on each festooned bough are seen
Young minstrel birds at play.

Aloe Vera
The Wand of Heaven

Aloe Vera: (Aloe.barbadensis)

Clump forming perennial succulent with basal rosettes of tapering, thick, sword-shaped leaves, mottled green, later greygreen. Flower stems carry bell shaped, yellow flowers in summer. Native to southern Africa, Arabia, and the Cape Verde Islands, this genus comprises of 325 species of tender, evergreen perennials, shrubs, trees and climbers. Introduced to Europe in the 10th century. (Family: Liliaceae/Aloeaceae)

The old ancient civilisations knew a lot about the virtues of the plants growing in their environment and many of the great minds belonging to those societies recorded the amazing benefits they discovered Aloe Vera had for mankind. From Persia and Egypt to the Middle East, to Greece, Italy, India and the African continent, her praises were, and still are, sung.

Aloe Vera, it could be said, is the oldest flowering plant on the planet Earth, for now. Discoveries in China of flowering plant fossils, in 1998, have dated this type of plant to between 142 to 148 million years old!

To survive on the Earth for that long, any living thing would need to evolve well enough to meet nature's challenges and perhaps that is why Aloe Vera has developed so many healing and life giving properties. In 1994, a Dr. Winters of the University of Texas health Science Centre, reported that Aloe contains at least 140 substances which control cell growth and division, reduce inflammation, stimulate the growth of white cells and other immune-function cells. Aloe heals wounds and is also an infection healer. Dr. Winters calls Aloe "a pharmacy in a plant."

And, over thousands of years, this wonderful succulent has had many names. Names that reflect the belief in both her healing and cosmetic uses. She's been known as 'The Wand of Heaven,' 'The Plant of Immortality,' 'Heaven's Blessing,' 'The Miracle Plant,' and, 'The Silent Healer.' The word 'Aloe' comes from the Arabic word 'Alloeh,' meaning 'bitter,' owing to the bitter liquid found in Aloe's leaves.

The earliest recorded reference to Aloe Vera is noted on the Sumerian clay tablets, which are over four thousand years old, and were found during excavations in the ancient city of Nippur. The tablets describe Aloe's whose leaves were used as a laxative.

Ever since then, over the ages, references can be found on the materials of the day, written by the great minds of all these times, touting the benefits of Aloe.

To the Egyptians, she was the plant of immortality and her magic healing effects were worshipped as a god. Aloe was used in the embalming of the Pharaohs by them and Cleopatra and Neferetiti regarded her gel as a fountain of youth and used it to protect their skin.

Her fame for healing wounds, convinced Aristotle to persuade Alexander the Great to capture the island of Socrotra, in the Indian Ocean, where so many of these fragrant desert lilies grew, so that he may obtain the plants and use them to treat his wounded soldiers.

From as early as 400 BC, the Aloe plant has been processed and exported to Asia. Since then, she has been grown in India for her healing properties and is still used today for these purposes, including a new method of the use of her leaves which are baked into bread to relieve mental illness.

According to the Bible too, Aloe was an embalming ingredient and the body of Jesus Christ was wrapped in linen impregnated with myrrh and aloes. (St. John 19:39.40).

To the Chinese, Aloe Vera is 'Lu Hui,' and they have been using this remarkable plant for at least 2,000 years. Today, they use it as a treatment for radiation burns, thermal burns, chapped and dry skin, leg ulcers and to help heal disorders of the stomach, spleen and liver.

In ancient Greek pharmacology, Dioscorides gives the first detailed description of Aloe Vera where he notes how her juice had the 'power of binding and inducing sleep,' whereas the whole leaf, 'could stop bleeding of many wounds.'

Additionally, Aloe is used around the world in a

plethora of cosmetics and is consumed as a healthy drink.
Today, serious studies of Aloe Vera are taking place
because this plant's leaves can seemingly help almost any
ailment, externally and internally, in relation to nearly
every part of the body, from bruises to H.I.V.

In the old days, Aloe was said to have the powers of
luck and protection and some believed, and some still do,
that an Aloe plant in the home guards against evil
influences and prevents accidents.

She can ease the pain of body and mind, and if you
can't grow one in your garden, try growing one in your
greenhouse. Ancient amongst the flowers, the fragrant
Aloe Vera, magnificent gift from nature, is truly *The Wand
from Heaven.*

Anemone
The Bride of the West Wind

Anemone: (Ranunculaceae)

*A perennial found throughout N. temperate and arctic regions -
flowers with 5 - 9 perianth - segments ranging from white to
yellow, pink or blue, but hybrids exhibit an even greater range
of colour: the flower stalks have small divided leaves two thirds
of the way up, basal leaves appear later. Family: Ranunculaceae. Over 150
species, Hepatica nobilis has a long history of medicine in Europe.*

The fragile and pretty Anemone derives its name from
the Greek 'anemos,' signifying the wind. For the
Greeks, Anemone was the bride of the west wind. At one
time Anemone was on of the favourite nymphs of
Chloris, queen of flowers, who, jealous of the attention
Zephyr, the wind god paid to the graceful nymph,
banished Anemone from her Court.
Zephyr turned her into a flower he could caress.

In olden times, wonderful powers were attributed to
Anemone. Magicians ordered that every person should
gather the first Anemone that he saw in the year as a
remedy against disease, a tradition which continued in
Britain for many a year.

To the Dutch, she is the Easter flower, as she is to the
French, when wearing her purple blooms, and in

Palestine, where she wears red, Anemone is said to have originated from the drops of blood that flowed from the wounds of Christ at the time of the Crucifixion, which accounts for Anemone being one
of the flowers chosen by the Christian Church as a symbol of the Holy Trinity.

At the approach of rain, or night, the delicately tissued petals of the wind flower are curled up as she goes to sleep and this is said to be the wood fairy nestling inside the flower and drawing the petals closely around itself.

The blooms of Anemone decked the halls of Venus and one old classic legend tells how, as Venus, mourning her beloved Adonis, wanders through the woodlands, Zephyr, god of wind, said to produce fruit and flowers from the sweetness of his breath, watches Venus from afar, and is so moved by her sorrow, that he turns each crystal tear into a flower as it falls to earth:

"Wind flowers, we since these blossoms call,
So very frail are they,
Tear-drop from Venus' eye let fall,
Our wood anemone."

Angelica
Flower of the Angels

Angelica: (Umbelliferae)

This is a genus of about 50 biennials native to temperate parts of the Northern Hemisphere. Can be found in northern and Eastern Europe, Greenland and central Asia. Aromatic, with thick hollow stems and deeply divided leaves, Angelica produces umbels of tiny green-white flowers that appear in early summer. Stems have culinary usage and when crystallised may be used for confectionery decoration.

Angelica's tiny blooms appear at the time of the Feast of the Annunciation which celebrates the angel Gabriel's foretelling to Mary of the birth of Jesus and of the promise of his greatness.

According to legend, the archangel Michael appeared to a medieval monk and told him about the healthy and protective properties of this wonderful plant. Her name comes from the Medieval Latin, 'herba angelica,' meaning 'angel herb,' from the belief that it would protect against evil and cure all ills. St. Michael is one of the four archangels in both Jewish and Christian scriptures. He is considered the patron angel and guardian of Israel. A feast honouring St. Michael, (Michaelmas) is held on November 8th.

Angelica did not cure the plague, but to protect

themselves against it, people would place a piece of the plant's root inside the mouth as an antiseptic and it is said that Angelica protected entire villages during the plague.

The word 'angel' from the Greek, refers to the 'messenger,' who was God's envoy to man and a divine link with the world of spirit. Serving God in various capacities, such as acting as a messenger or as a guardian of individuals, angels, in traditional Christianity, were understood to be created before
the world and are often depicted with a human body and wings. This concept began in the Hebrew Bible or Old Testament.

This link between heaven and earth can be seen in many graveyards where angels are depicted in many shapes and forms. Having guarded a person during their lifetime, an angel's presence on a grave intimates that protection continues in death. Angels are often seen as symbols of innocence and virtue.

Many religions believe in similar beings. In some primitive religions, legends tell of bright, powerful spirits that appear in dreams or visions and who protect people and tribes. In Hinduism and Buddhism, many major gods are accompanied by a band of spiritual beings. The Islamic belief in angels
resembles that of Judaism and Christianity where some angels are placed near God and others are given special duties.

A gift from the angels, Angelica is used in many parts of the world for medicinal purposes and as an essential oil in perfumes. Her leaves are used for herbal tea, to decorate food, and the fragrance of them is said to smell like that of an angel's! Her seeds are used for making candy and her stalks for making jam.

Chinese medicine uses at least ten varieties of Angelica, to strengthen the heart and immune system. One form of Angelica – Angelica.sinensis – is probably the most important Chinese tonic after Ginseng, dating back to about AD200.

Angelica is now a component of many Chinese medicines in Hong Kong, San Francisco, Singapore as well as China.

In Europe during the 15th century, Angelica was rated the most important of all medicinal herbs. In England, dried Angelica roots helped painful stomachs and abated lust!

Around the world, various types of Angelica are used mainly as a tonic for women. Although not given to pregnant women, chicken soup with Angelica root is a popular folk remedy after childbirth.

All parts of the plant were believed once to be effective against spells and enchantment. In Germany, where Angelica was known as The Root of the Holy Ghost, people believed that the plant could eliminate the effects of intoxication and render witchcraft harmless.

For protection against witchcraft, Angelica was once worn against the body and placed around the house. To protect the house and its inhabitants from evil of all kinds, Angelica was planted in the garden at all Four Corners of the house.

American Indians too, used Angelica for medicinal

purposes and if Angelica is included amongst the dried herbs and flowers in a Dream Pillow, it is believed by some that it will give a pleasant, relaxing sleep.

Associated with divine magic and inspiration, our gardens can only be enhanced by the presence of the amazing and useful Angelica, the flower of the angels.

Aster
Starflowers from Teardrops

Aster: (Compositae)

Aster is a member of a large group of mainly perennials from America, Asia and Africa, whose flower heads are daisy-like with outer ray florets of blue, pink, purple, or white. Flowering later than most perennials they continue to colour our gardens brightly until late autumn. (Genus: Aster, over 250 species. Family: Compositae.) Commonly known as Michaelmas Daisy and Starwort.

According to the Victorian writers of the language of flowers, the heart-cheering Aster is the symbol of love, daintiness, and was once a talisman of love.

But in the early days, to the ancients, Asters were thought to hold magical powers. People of old used to burn the leaves of Aster, believing the odour would drive away serpents and evil spirits.

Her name, Aster, means 'star,' and according to one story, this beautiful flower originates from the tears of Astraea, the Greek goddess of justice, daughter of Zeus and Themis. The god Jupiter, was so angered once by people fighting each other with iron weapons, he decided to send a great flood to destroy the entire race.

All the gods left the Earth and the last to leave was Astraea, who was so saddened at having to go that she asked to be turned into a star. When, eventually, the waters receded, all that could be seen was mud and slime. Astraea was so sorrowful when she looked down and saw how Earth had lost its beauty, she wept tears of stardust, and where each rainbow particle touched the Earth, a lovely starflower appeared and they were named Aster, in honour of the goddess.

To the English, Aster was known once as Starwort, owing to the healing properties of the flower's root. The purple Aster is cultivated by the Chinese for medicinal use and was first mentioned in Chinese literature c.AD200. The purple Aster is found in meadows and beside rivers in Eastern Asia.
Virgil wrote that the flavour of honey would be improved if Aster flowers were boiled in wine and placed near a beehive. This association between the Aster and honeybees continues in herbal medicine today where the Aster is used as an expectorant herb with honey to help clear the bronchial system of infection.

The Cherokee Indians tell a different story about the origins of Aster. According to one of their legends, two warring tribes once battled over a hill and down into a village, where all the villagers were killed except two little sisters who hid in the woods. The sisters both wore skin dresses, one dyed
lavender-blue with fringes, the other bright yellow.

When it was safe to leave the woods, the two sisters sought out the herb woman who lived over the mountain in another valley. The herb woman gathered herbs by day and made magic potions at night.

One night, as the sisters slept, the herb woman looked into the future and saw that the enemy would hunt down the two girls. So, she sprinkled them with a magic brew and covered them with leaves.

In the morning there were two flowers where the little sisters had once been. One was the lavender-blue Aster; the other was the yellow Golden-rod.

Also known as Michaelmas Daisy, this name was given first to a North American species when the Gregorian Calendar was introduced which brought Michaelmas forward by 11 days, to 29th September, the time of flowering.

Wreaths of Asters were once placed on the altars of the gods and owing to her association with love, the Aster is also known as the herb of Venus. To the French, the Aster is their flower emblem, to the Chinese, she signifies fidelity.

Whether they grow in meadows or mountains, near rivers or fountains, the rainbow-coloured starflowers of Aster are a heavenly vision and a grace to every garden.

The Broom
Chosen Flower of a Princely Race

The Scottish Broom: (Cytisus scoparius)

More than 100 species of this attractive shrub grow in Europe, Asia, and Africa. The Scottish Broom, (Cytisus scoparius), is grown in the United States. Many of its branches are leafless or almost without leaves. The showy yellow flowers are shaped like butterflies, the fruit is a pod with one or more seeds in it. The Broom is a member of the pea family. Some types of Broom are used as dyes. Family: Leguminoseae.

To the travelling people of Scotland, the sight of the bright yellow blossoms of the Broom, announces the advent of Spring, and, stirs the wandering hearts to move on.

And, without fail too, as though whispered to them by the wind, the wild mountain goats know the Broom has begun to flower, and they come down from the mountains to eat the first young blooms.

The Broom's connection with royalty originates from the royal house of the Plantagenet's, whose crest was a genet passing between two sprigs of Broom, and who took their name from the Latin, "Planta genista," which means "sprig of the broom plant."

According to tradition, as Count Geoffrey of Anjou, leading his troops to battle, passed through a rocky gorge, he remarked how on the other side, bushes of full blossomed glory, clung with firm grasps to the stones, yet upheld the loosened soil. "This plant," he cried, "shall be my cognizance! I will carry it in my crest upon the battlefield, at tournament, and when dispensing justice."

He placed a sprig of Broom, into the helmet of his armour, and midst the battle, Geoffrey the Brave cried "Planta genista!" and his men echoed, "Planta genista!" as they drove back the foe. After the battle, Count Geoffrey took the name of Plantagenet, which he passed to his descendants. The name was carried proudly from Henry II to Richard III, who was the last branch of Anjou.

Legend in England states that witches were supposed to love the Broom and to use it for riding about at midnight.

In some parts of Scotland, the golden blooms are considered to be a sign of plentiful crops, when the Broom is fully blossomed early.

Beloved by the bee and the butterfly, this glorious golden vision, in its more humble profession, employed as a broom, is symbolic of 'humility.'

Carnation
The Flower that Decked the Crowns

Carnation:(Dianthus caryophyllaceous)

A perennial species of pink native to the Mediterranean leaves tufted, flowers with spreading, slightly frilly petals. Wild carnations have pink, strongly scented flowers. Ornamental hybrids and garden cultivars are various colours, and may have multiple petals.

Associated with January, dedicated to Jupiter by the Greeks, few flowers have attained such a high distinction as the Carnation. Loved by the ancients for its divine perfume, the Carnation was given place of honour *"to deck the crowns of pleasure,"* hence the origin of the name.

In old Saxon the spelling means "coronation." Owing to the spice giving properties, the Carnation was in earlier times, used to impart flavour to wine and ale. The wine presented to brides after the wedding ceremony was always especially flavoured with Carnation and was worn by betrothed lovers to mark their mutual engagement.

In Italy, the Carnation is a favourite, where it represents Ardent Love. The flower is also dedicated to

St. Peter and his day, (June 29th,) is known as the Day of the Carnations.

An Italian legend, referring to the Carnation, tells the story of Margherita, who loved a brave and chivalrous knight name Orlando. Their marriage was already fixed when Orlando was called to do battle. On taking his leave from her, Orlando begged her to give him the white Carnation she wore. Margherita put the Carnation in a silken bag, and after she had fastened it on him, the brave knight gave her one last embrace.

A year later, a horseman brought Margherita the sad news of Orlando's death and returned the silken bag to her. Now the only thing remaining of her precious love, Margherita treasured the little silken bag. On opening it one day, she noticed that the once white Carnation had a deep crimson hue, dyed by her lover's blood, but also some tiny seeds. These she planted, and soon, to her joy, some tiny shoots appeared which later developed into a strong Carnation with tightly rolled up buds. But the day the flowers opened, Margherita's loving care was rewarded with wonder, for each flower was quite different from the original, it's centre was marked by a deep crimson stain, like the blood which had stained Orlando's withered blossom. To Margherita, this was confirmation of their true and faithful love. Thereafter, she tended the precious flowers, never marrying, and when she died, she left the Carnation as a legacy to her sisters, with instructions never to give one of its blooms to anyone except their one true love. The plant became a family heirloom with every daughter born into the family being given at birth a vase containing the white and crimson Carnation. If a girl in the house never married, the plant would wither and die.

Carnation is still very much a favourite flower of gardeners today and popularly used as a wedding flower and for bouquets and garlands. Many of this flower's species are grown for their summer fragrances.

Chamomile
The Plant's Physician

Chamomile: (Chamaemelum)

*Compositae/Asteraceae, Chamomil.nobile – Anthemis nobilis
(Roman Chamomile). Mat forming evergreen perennial with
aromatic, finely divided leaves up to 2 inches long. Long
stalked, solitary flowers with yellow discs and creamy white ray
florets appearing in summer, 6 – 8 ins. Containing only four
species this genus is native to Europe and Mediterranean
regions.*

The monks of the middle ages first noted the
remarkable properties of bright Chamomile and they
noted with amazement how ailing or sickly plants often
recovered fully when this wonderful, long stalked daisy
was planted near them. But Chamomile's properties were
known to man for thousands of years before the Middle
Ages and this plant, it seems, has always been held in high
esteem.

In the 9th century, the Anglo Saxons added
Chamomile to their ritual baths in order to attract love.
Chamomile is listed in one of their poems, Lacnunga, as
one of the nine sacred herbs given to mankind by Woden.
It was thought that dried

Chamomile, sprinkled around property, could remove curses and bad spells and its association with luck led to gamblers washing their hands with it to ensure winnings.

The ancient Egyptians revered Chamomile and dedicated the daisy to their gods. Garlands created from Chamomile's flowers were draped over statues of Egyptian deities in King Tut's tomb and powdered flowers were sprinkled into the mummy of Ramesis the 2nd to act as an insecticide.

The name Chamomile comes from the Greek chamaimelon, which means "apple on the ground" and refers to the strong apple scent of the foliage when trodden upon.

Chamomile's association with tea was popularised by Beatrix Potter but there is no doubt that Chamomile has been a favourite drink since before the Chinese made the first ever cup of tea in 2737BC!

In May 1950, two brothers from Tolland, Denmark, discovered a body, 2,400 years old, in a peat bog. Scientists revealed that his last meal was a soup made from vegetables and seeds, some cultivated and some wild, as well as barley, linseed, knotweed, bristle-grass and Chamomile. Tollund man's body is kept in the Silkeborg Museum in Denmark.

The value of Chamomile as a medicinal herb is widely known and she is also popular for beauty purposes. Chamomile's flowers brighten, lighten and condition blonde hair. In summer they are gathered for oil, or dried for use in infusions, dermatological creams, and are lovely

for pot pourri and herb pillows. Burned alone,
Chamomile will help induce
sleep and tired eyes can be soothed by washing them in
Chamomile tea.

To many, Chamomile symbolises sleep, meditation,
money, purification and luck. To your garden,
Chamomile, the plant's physician, and her beautiful little
daisies, will bring protection.

Christmas Rose
Blossoms Amidst the Snow

Helleborous Niger: (Ranunculaceae).

Genus of perennials, some of which are evergreen, grown for their winter and spring flowers. Flowers in a variety of colours from purple to green, yellow-white. Helleborous.argutifolous, for example, has cup shaped pale yellow flowers. Helleborous.Niger is the species commonly known as The Christmas Rose. Over twenty species are in cultivation in Europe and Asia. Helleborous.Niger and Helleborous.foetidus are native in Western European woodlands.

The glorious sight of her pure white blossoms appearing in the cold depths of winter cannot fail to warm our hearts and has earned the beautiful Helleborous.niger the name of Christmas Rose.

Used by mankind since the Neolithic period, it's not surprising that these old ancestors of ours believed that the Christmas Rose had magical properties when they discovered her blossoms amidst the snow in their woodlands at the rarest time of flowering. Prehistoric burial chambers sometimes contain seed and capsules from this plant and it is believed that it may have been used by these early people for religious and medical purposes and as a poison for their arrows since all parts of the Christmas Rose are poisonous. The Gauls, too, used this plant for their arrows.

The knowledge of this deadly aspect of the Christmas Rose passed down through the ages and fourteen hundred years before Christ was born, to the ancient Greeks, the Christmas Rose was known as Melampode. This former name was derived by Pliny from the name Melampos, a mythical Greek soothsayer and healer. Melampos used this plant as a herb to cure the madness of King Proteus' daughters and other Greek women who lost their hair and roamed wildly in the mountains and deserts of Tiryns!

The ancient Greeks also made use of the plants' toxic properties and used it to poison the wells of their enemies. To them, the Melampode was associated with demons and possession.

The secret origins of this wonderful winter flower have fascinated people beyond memory and one tradition declares that in the days of Adam and Eve, this plant first blossomed in the gardens of heaven where it was known by the angels who tended it as "the rose of love."

One cold winter, when Adam and Eve's garden lay shrouded in snow, and not one of the many coloured blossoms attended by them remained to tint the whiteness of their paradise, the angels noticed how sad they looked in Eden. Taking pity on them, they asked the Almighty to be allowed to carry their pure celestial flower to the unhappy couple as a token of His love and mercy and of a brighter future. So came the first of this species to Earth.

Another legend tells how Hellebore came to be known by its common name today. The Christmas Rose. According to this well known legend, a poor shepherd maiden named Madelon wept by the entrance to the cattle shed where the baby Jesus' manger was. As she watched the three kings offer the sleeping Saviour their gifts of frankincense, Myrrh and gold, she wished that she could give a gift to Him. An angel passing noticed the girl, and, clearing some snow, revealed to the girl the beautiful blossoms of the rose of love. The poor shepherdess offered them as a token to the Christ child and they then became known as the Christmas Rose.

From these old times, well into the 17th century, the Christmas Rose continued to be used as a cure for madness, melancholy and hypochondria. Folk tradition around Europe records how people used to plant the Christmas Rose near their cottage doors as a protection from evil spells and once blessed their cattle with it. French tradition tells of a sorcerer scattering dried powdered Hellebore in the air to make himself invisible. In France today, this plant is known as Rose-de-Noel or Flower of the Nativity.

In medieval times, the Christmas Rose was known as the "flower of St.Agnes" having been dedicated to her on account of the purity of its blossoms.

Regarded of an emblem of purity, the Christmas Rose, the last flower of the year, heralds the new one with a flourish of pink tinged waxy petals, a symbol of promise.

No gardener need go far to find

The Christmas Rose
The fairest of the flowers that mark
The sweet year's close.

December. Dollie Radford. (1858-1920)

Chrysanthemum
Flower of Happiness

Chrysanthemum: (Dandrathema)

Chrysanthemum:(Compositae) is native to Europe, Asia, and North America. A group of strongly scented shrubby herbs, grown for their beautiful and abundant blossoms which usually appear in autumn. Chrysanthemum blossoms are made up of many flowers and careful de-budding may produce flowers of up to eight inches across. Blossoms range from white or yellow to pink or red. A favourite of gardeners, Chrysanthemum comes in many flower forms, now classified botanically under Dandrathema. Flower forms are:- **Incurved:** *(Fully double)* **Fully Reflexed:** *(double flowers with curved petals)* **Reflexed:** *(with petals that form and umbrella like shape)* **Single:** *(flowers open, each have about 5 rows of flat petals)* **Pompom:** *(fully double, dense spherical flowers with tubular petals)* **Anemone-centred:** *(single flowers with dome shaped central disc), and* **Spoon-type:** *(similar to single form but with tubular ray petals at the tips that spread out)*

The amazing and colourful Chrysanthemum is one of the beloved flowers of gardeners in temperate climates because she comes in so many pleasing and lovely forms.

To the Japanese though, she is the sacred symbol of the birth of the old Empire of Japan. One legend tells how once, twelve young maidens and young men left China and set sail on a journey to find the herb of youth. They had heard that this herb could bring eternal youth and, to trade for it, they took with them baskets full of Chrysanthemum plants.

During their journey, disaster struck and they became shipwrecked near what they thought was an uninhabited island. Fortunately, they were able to swim ashore and they gathered up the floating baskets of Chrysanthemums and planted them all over the island as happy thanks for their safety. That island was Japan and since then, for hundreds of years, Japan's imperial emblem has featured a golden Chrysanthemum with sixteen petals. The flower is also carved on the throne of The Japanese Emperor.

In 797, the ruler of Japan, the Mikado, made Chrysanthemum his personal emblem and decreed that it could only be used by royalty. Today, the Supreme Order of the Chrysanthemum is still Japan's highest award and is given to Japanese royalty, nobility, and male foreign heads of state. The
Feast of the Chrysanthemums is held in Japan in October. Japan could be the world's greatest grower of Chrysanthemums since their introduction to Japan in the 4th century from China.

However, she has been cultivated in China for more than two thousand years and is known in some places as 'The Flower of the East' and 'The Flower of Life.' In China during the 400's, Tao Yuanming, became a famous breeder of her blossoms and after his death, his native city was named Juxian, which means 'City of Chrysanthemums.'

The petals of Chrysanthemum are eaten in China to encourage longevity and a tea made from her flowers is said to be a cure for headaches and depression. According to Chinese Feng Shui, Chrysanthemums bring happiness to your home.

Europeans too, love her beautiful blossoms but before 1500, she was known to the British as 'Corn Marigold.' After that date, when Britain began importing her oriental form from the Far East, the name changed to 'Chrysanthemum,' which is derived from the Greek words meaning 'golden flower.'

A European legend in relation to her white blossom, tells the story of a poor family who once lived in the Black Forest in Germany. They had just sat down to a simple meal, on Christmas Eve, when they heard a cry from outside their door. When they opened the door, they found a man who was blue with the cold. Hastily, they wrapped him in blankets and brought him inside to share their food. Once warmed and well, the man shed the blankets and before them he sat in shining white clothes with a divine halo around his head. Smiling as he left, he revealed to them that he was Jesus Christ himself.

The next morning, when they opened their door, two Chrysanthemums wearing the colour white grew where he had stood. Today, many Germans bring white Chrysanthemums into their homes at Christmas Eve.

Over her long history, she has been associated with life's many positive aspects according to her beautiful colours. In general, Chrysanthemum symbolises abundance and wealth, cheerfulness and friendship. Her red blossoms represent 'love,' white blossoms represent 'truth,' and the Chinese Chrysanthemum is associated with 'Cheerfulness under adversity.'

The beauty and colour of her many forms never fails to bring joy and make us smile. She is a true flower of happiness, Chrysanthemum.

Clematis
The Plant of the Bohemians

Clematis: (Ranunculaceae)

Genus of evergreen or deciduous, mainly twining climbers and herbaceous perennials, cultivated for their mass of flowers, often followed by decorative seed heads, and grown on walls and trellises and together with trees, shrubs and other host plants. Most have bell shaped flowers usually with four to six petals, or flattish flowers. Fully to half hardy.

Clematis could be described today as the flower of many faces and seasons, considering that there are up to one hundred late flowering varieties, as well as more than thirty large late flowering hybrids, along with spring and summer varieties, providing our gardens with visions of glorious colour, shape and cheer nearly all year round. No wonder Clematis is such a favourite!

Once known as the "Wild Vine," one of the originals, with its far reaching foliage and exquisite white blooms, was a favourite flower in its natural British home. In warmer climates, you will find Clematis happily growing lovely purple blossoms as she climbs trees, clambers over shrubs and clings onto stronger plants. Clematis originated in many regions of mountainous Europe and North America and is also known as "travellers' joy," but in old Russia, she was the "Plant of the Bohemians," Tziganka.

The Russian legend that accounts for the name tells how once, the Cossacks were at war with the Tartars and on one occasion, finding the latter too strong for them, turned to run away. The Cossack leader, ashamed, struck his own forehead with the handle of his pike, and instantly, a violent hurricane arrived which whirled his cowardly comrades in the air, pounded them into a thousand fragments, and mingled their dust with that of their enemy, the Tartars.

From this dust, emerged Tziganka,(Clematis,) but so troubled were the souls of the Cossacks, knowing their bones were mingled with the earth of the foreigners, that they prayed to God to scatter the dust from their bodies at home, in their beloved Ukraine, where young girls could pluck and weave into garlands the flowers of the Tziganka.

God heard them and granted the patriotic prayer, and it was a popular belief in that part of Russia that if every man would hang a Tziganka from his waist belt, all the dead Cossacks would again come to life.

The red blossomed Clematis, with its sweet perfume, was given the name of "ladies bower" and "virgin bower" to compliment Queen Elizabeth, the "virgin Queen." But Clematis is also fabled to have been given that name in honour of the Virgin Mary because several times the plant had provided her with grateful shade when resting with the infant Jesus on her journeys to Egypt.

She has earned the beautiful emblem of rest and consolation, and it is surely understandably deserved, for whether she is cascading like a waterfall of colour from wire, or shining up pergolas, Clematis gladdens our hearts with her prolific and welcoming wave.

The Cornflower
True Blue Beauty

Cornflower: (Centaurea.cyanus)

Blue Cornflower,(compositae family). A genus of annuals and perennials grown for their thistle like centres, which are surrounded by slender ray petals. Fully hardy, Blue Cornflower has lance shaped grey green leaves and blue flowers in Summer and early Autumn.

Growing wild in and around the cornfields of Europe and the United States, wonderful blue cornflowers add vibrant and lively colour to the countryside as they nod and dance in the wind. Just as Autumn and Summer begin to change places; just before harvest begins, when all that was green turns to gold, the true blue blossoms appear.

Originating in Europe, the Blue Cornflower has been a part of our gardens for centuries, indeed, since ancient times, and its genus name, Centaurea, comes from 'Kentauros,' the Greek name for a Thessalonian tribe of expert horseman, the Centaurs.

In Greek mythology, a centaur was a creature with the arms, head and torso of a man and the body and legs of a horse. The most famous of the centaurs, Chiron, who acted as teacher to Jason, Achilles, and many other Greek Heroes, used the Blue
Cornflower to cure himself of a wound he sustained from an arrow. The arrow was poisoned with the blood of the monster known as the one hundred headed Hydra. So Chiron was credited for discovering the healing properties of the Blue Cornflower and the plant was named after him.

To the French, she is known as bluet and to the English she is blue-blow. The Scots call her Blue Bonnet but the most common name for the Blue Cornflower is Bachelor Buttons which refers to a time when it was placed in the buttonholes of the suits or shirts of bachelors when they went courting.

Throughout history the Blue Cornflower has been connected to romance and the beautiful colour of her blossoms are said to be emblematic of delicate sympathy that feeds on hope. Wilhelm, the King of Prussia and first Emperor of United Germany, made the Blue Cornflower, "die Kornblume," his emblem in memory of a special time for him during the Napoleonic wars. His mother, Queen Louisa of Prussia, was forced out of Berlin and she fled with her children and hid in a cornfield. To help her children to stay still and quiet, she sat with them in the corn weaving garlands out of Blue Cornflowers and Wilhelm never forgot that time.

This beautiful flower is also the national flower of Estonia where it has been associated with wealth because it grows best in the richest fields of grain.

The second part of the Blue Cornflower's genus name, Cyanus, is said to have been given by the Roman goddess of flowers, Flora in honour of a young devotee of this name. According to Roman mythology, every day while the flowers lasted, Cyanus laid a wreath of them at Flora's shrine. Cyanus was so devoted to the goddess that he would scarcely ever leave the cornfields.

One morning they found him dead, stretched upon the field, half-woven garlands of his favourite blossoms scattered all around. When Flora head about this she commanded that the flowers so fondly loved by the faithful Cyanus should henceforth be called by his name. Flora's major festivals were celebrated in the spring months from 28th April – early May and known as Floralia.

A similar tale is told in Russia, about a time when once the water nymph Rusalka, a goddess of nature, left her river to wander in the fields. Now she did this quite often, always returning to the water before her hair was entirely dry, but on this occasion she spied the youth Basilek upon the road and instantly fell in love with him. When Basilek noticed her and saw her beautiful form and long flowing hair, he returned a look of love to her so she laughed and ran back into the cornfields.

Basilek immediately ran after her following the sounds of her melodic laughter and she allowed herself to be captured. Basilek forgot all the warnings he had heard about pursuing those of the aquatic race and they both fell together in the field, rolling and laughing, then she began tickling him relentlessly until he could no longer breathe and so he died from her seduction. Rusalka felt so sad for what she had done that she turned Basilek into the first of all Blue Cornflowers, so, still, in some Slavic countries the Blue Cornflower is known as "Basilek."

The blossoms of the Blue Cornflower are long lasting and make excellent cut flowers as well as adding a brilliance of colour to any floral display of dried flowers. In the wild flower section of our gardens they look so pretty alongside their pink cousins. But there is no better sight of this true blue beauty than the one where she's growing at home amidst the cornfields.

The Daisy
The Day's Eye

The Daisy:(Bellis perennis)

*A perennial native to Europe and W.Asia), with a basal rosette
of oval or spoon-shaped leaves: leafless flowering stems up to 20cm, each bearing
a solitary flower-head, outer ray florets white often tinge red, inner disc florets
yellow.*

No flower perhaps, has been more universally sung and praised by poets than the beautiful humble Daisy. In early times, the Daisy signified womanly truth, purity and fidelity, and patient endurance. Being a flower of light, open, it is the emblem of the soul, closed, it is the emblem of purity.

Held in high esteem throughout Europe, this cheerful flower, whose home is everywhere, blooms month in, month out, although it is associated with April.

For the Italians, the Daisy is a sacred flower. It is the star of Italy, symbol of Queen Margherita. The Welsh give it the lovely name of "trambling star," and in Scotland, its blossoms are fondly called "bairns flowers." The use of the Daisy's petals as a means to discover the measure of love bestowed on young girls by their lovers, gave it the name in Germany, of "love's measure." This custom prevails in many countries where the Daisy is seen as a little love token.

The Saxon name for the common Daisy, is "day's eye." A beautiful and apt name for this little flower. They took note of how at sunset the flower closed its petals over its yellow centre, its "eye," to unfold them again at dawn, as if it were reopening the eye. Appearing to them, refreshed after what seemed a good night's sleep, the flower prompted them to describe someone who enjoyed a good rest as feeling "as fresh as a daisy."

According to legend, the Daisy owes its origin to a daughter of the goddess Belus, who with her sister dryads presided over woodlands. One day, as this dainty nymph dances with her favoured lover Ephigeus, so sweet does she appear, so fresh, that she attracts the attention of Vertumnia, guardian deity of spring and of orchards, who flies to her side. Ephigeus, heart full of jealous rage, turns wrathfully on Vertumnia, and pretty Bellis, fearful of her own and her lover's safety, transforms herself into a flower, the Daisy.

These beauties continue to please us with their presence until the first snows, and thankfully, no matter how often we cut the grass, the enduring Daisy pops right back up!

Forget-Me-Not
Blossoms of Heaven

Forget-Me-Not: Myosotis (Boraginaceous)

Genus of annuals, bi-annuals and perennials, grown for their flowers. Has oval, rough textured leaves and in spring and summer, tight sprays of open funnel-shaped, tiny yellow, white or blue flowers with a yellow centre. Found wild in North
America, Europe and New Zealand.

The romantic Forget-Me-Not has long since been associated with love, truth, and remembrance. A low growing plant of the borage family, Forget-Me-Not is a popular ornamental. Her name, which is mid 16th century, translates from the old French name ne m'oubliez mye and is said to have the virtue of ensuring the wearer of the flower would never be forgotten by a lover.

One variety, Myosotis alpestris, a beautiful Forget Me-Not with tiny sky blue blossoms, is Alaska's state flower, but wherever this lovely plant grows, she is emblematic of love.

Some Pacific Northwest Native Americans used Forget-Me-Not as a love charm and to Italians, she is the "little love flower" that is the embodiment of a young maiden who was drowned and transformed into a Forget-Me-not.

Found on wet banks and in the shallow waters of ponds, many of Forget-me-not's myths are stories set near rivers or pools.

One story, from Massachusetts, tells how Forget-Me-Nots once grew in a little marsh at the summit of Egg Rock, three miles off of the Nahant shore. It was believed that if a girl should receive one of these little flowers from her lover, the two would be faithful to each other through all their married life.

One day, a couple strolled together on the Nahant cliffs and the young man remembered the legend of the Forget-Me- Not and offered to gather some of them for his young lady as a memento. Eagerly, he ran down to his boat, pushed out, and headed towards the rock, unaware that a storm was brewing. As his boat neared Egg Rock, the waves were running high and the wind freshened as the sun sank. Other sailors who had come ashore, stood with his love and watched aghast as the little boat in the distance first seemed to disappear, and then crashed against the rock of its destination. The following day, the young man's body was washed ashore, and a bunch of Forget-Me-Nots was clasped in his rigid hand.

In the days of the old Knights, Forget-Me-Nots were woven into their collars to keep their love with them when they went of to war, and a Flemish legend tells how Forget-Me-Nots first sprang upon the plain from the seed of a small spray carried by an Englishman who fell in the Battle of Waterloo.

An old tradition in relation to herbal uses of the early 1900's states that the juice of Forget-me-Not could harden steel and helped respiratory problems if used as a syrup, and Native Americans once used the little plant to treat dog and snake bits.

The origin of Forget-Me-Not's name was thought to have come from Henry the fourth of England who took this plant for his emblem, but Christian tradition tells a different story. When Adam finished naming the plants in the Garden of Eden, the
Lord walked through it and pleased, stopped to look closer at a little plant with tiny flowers. He asked the plant what name it had been given and the plant was so scared that it said it had forgotten. The Lord continued his walk and later, at dusk, as he was leaving the divine garden, he passed the little plant again and said lovingly, "Goodnight. Forget-Me-Not."

The lovely Forget-Me-Not has inspired many poets and Longfellow wrote:-

"Silently, one by one, in the infinite meadows of heaven
Blossom the lovely stars, the Forget-Me-Nots of the Angels."

Heartsease
Kiss me at the Garden Gate

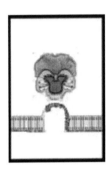

Heartsease: (viola tricolor)

A species of violet, the Heartsease is distinguished as the "field pansy." Also called "wild pansy," native to Europe. The flowers are blue, yellow, white, or a combination of these
colours.

No flower is, perhaps, a more popular favourite or has had so many fond names given to it, such as, "Kiss-me," "Kiss-me quick," "Kiss-me-at-the-garden-gate," "Cuddle-me," "Forgetme-not," and, says Shakespeare; "Maidens call it 'Love in idleness'" loving, that is, in vain.

Dedicated to St. Valentine, associated with February, Heartsease is emblematic of loving thoughts and of faithful remembrance.

According to an old legend, the Heartsease was at first milk-white, until struck by a blow from Cupid's bow, "which that mischievous little love god had aimed at stately Diana." Shakespeare calls it "Cupid's flower of purple dye," and endows it with magic properties.

This is the little western flower that the fairy King Oberon bids his page, Puck, fetch that he may drop the liquor of it on the closed eyes of the unconscious Titania.

Pensee, the French name for Heartsease, means, "a thought," and it signifies "think of me." In Italy and Spain, we find a similar name for the flower, pensiero, pensamento.

From the three colours in one bloom, the cheerful little Heartsease was known to the old herbalists as herba Trinitatis, Herb Trinity. One German legend, however, gives another origin of the name: At first the pansy owned a perfume even more delicious than her sister the sweet violet. It grew in fields and because it was so much sought after by the people, the precious corn and vegetables were being constantly trodden down. Now this so grieved the tender hearted flower, that it prayed to the Holy Trinity to take away some of its perfume. The prayer was granted and from that time the Heartsease has been known as Dreifaltigkeits Blume, or, "Flower of the Trinity."

Like the sweet violet, Heartsease emblemizes a happy trustfulness and "the content that is our best having."

Heather
For the Love of Mountain

Heather: (Calluna Vulgaris)

*(Family, Ericaceae), Calluna, Daboecia, and Erica. All
Calluna and Daboecia cultivars and most Erica species must be
grown in acid soil but otherwise Heather requires little
attention. There are whites, pinks and purple heathers that will
provide interest at all times of the year and provide excellent
ground cover. Calluna.vulgaris is a short to medium height
shrub, its leaves are in opposite rows and its flowers are
usually pale purple sitting in leafy stalked spikes. From June to
October all of Heather's habitats are swathed in rich purple,
pink or white and complement both summer and autumn.*

From late Summer to Autumn, on a fine day walking
in our hillsides, the sight of beautiful Heather's purple
cloak of blossoms stirs happiness within and evokes a
true feeling of constancy. And constant she is, for
wherever trees are cleared or fields are left uncultivated,
Heather makes her lovely appearance. Many tales are told
about this plant's usefulness to
humans, birds, and the bees, earning her divine
admiration from the beginning of human time.

Spread throughout Europe and North America,
Heather's tiny blossoms paint large areas of heath, hillside
and mountain in a range of colour and one tale, relating

to mountains, tells of a time when she had no blossoms at all.

According to that story, set only a little while after the Earth was made, the plants and trees were settling into the places where they wanted to grow and each was happy in its chosen home and with the colours and shapes of the blossoms nature had bestowed upon it. Except Heather. Heather wasn't sure where to go to play her part in Nature's provision because she had no flowers nor fragrance. However, she did her best to be contended and tried to remain bright and green on the ground.

One day, she heard the bare, rocky mountain ask if any of the plants would come and cover his rocks with their brightness and beauty to protect them from the cold. Each gave a reason why they couldn't. One could not leave the pond. One was required by the moss. Some could not leave the fields or forests. Heather trembled with eagerness and asked the mountain to consider her, saying that although she had no blossoms like the others, she would try and keep the wind and the sun away from the mountain. Mountain was delighted and little Heather soon covered the rock mountainside in bright green. Mountain sang her praises to the other plants who jealously sneered that she had no fragrant blossoms. Then, through the mist a sweet voice was heard saying that Heather, because she had loved and protected the lonely Mountain, would, before the day was out, be granted many coloured blossoms, and enough that would suit many living things so that the mountain would never be lonely again.

Throughout the ages, helpful Heather became useful for many of Man's needs, and she was considered one of their sacred, magical plants. Offerings were made to her at the festival of Beltane eve to attract good luck and Heather is the midsummer tree of the Summer Solstice.

Honey made from her blossoms is special and darker in colour and has been used for hundreds of years for medicinal purposes. In the old days, it was Heather honey that was one of the ingredients in the magic mead the old tribes made. Evidence of this beverage has been found on the Isle of Rum in
Scotland's West Coast, where a shard from the Neolithic period contained traces of fermented honey mead.
Heather ale is one of the oldest styles of ale in the world. It is having a revival at the present time but the secret of the ancient brand died with the
old tribes who refused to reveal it even to King James. A poem by Robert Louis Stevenson tells this story.

Heather's practical uses are many and she has been used as bedding, thatching for roofs, making ropes, as fuel, and for a vast array of medicinal purposes. Her roots can even be used for making musical pipes!
Gardeners have cultivated her many varieties for many years now and there is a wide range of species available with white flowers, and pinks, as well as purples. She is home to many species of birds and insects, companion to many alpine plants, but it is for the love of mountain that Heather is best known and how wonderful all mountains look when swathed in
her rich purple blossom.

Iris
Rainbow Flower!

Iris: (Iridaceae)

A perennial, sometimes evergreen, native to N temperate regions, divisible into two groups; those with rhizomes have sword-shaped leaves in flat fans; those with bulbs have leaves narrow, channelled, or cylindrical; flowers large, showy, the parts in threes and structurally complex, often in a combination of colours with conspicuous honey guides; fruit a capsule, sometimes with brightly coloured seeds. Many species and cultivars are grown for ornament. (Genus: Iris, 300 species. Family: Iridaceae.)

Originally named after Iris, the Greek Goddess of the rainbow, as their shades and markings are reminiscent of those of the rainbow, these beautiful flowers are emblematic of promise, light and hope, pride and bravery.

Iris is cultivated everywhere, it would seem, owing to the beauty and variety of its blooms. The Yellow Flag Iris grows wild now in the thousands in the West Highlands of Scotland.

A beautiful native American Iris, the iris hexagona, has large deep blue flowers, variegated with purple, white and yellow. The Germans have their native species too, iris

Germanica, and they used to plant it on the roofs of their cottages.

The Eastern nations regarded it with high esteem, the Egyptians placed Iris on the bow of the Sphinx and on the sceptres of the monarchs, regarding it as a symbol of power.

Several different species are still grown as a source of "orris," which is dried root of Iris. Orris contains a volatile oil, which gives a violet perfume that intensifies as the dried rhizome ages.

Widely used as a medicinal plant among native Americans, the Creek people grew Iris near their villages.

Iris, the goddess, was named after the rainbow, the messenger of the gods who was the bearer of good news. In Christian belief, the rainbow being God's radiant messenger, "And it shall come to pass, when I bring a cloud over the earth, that the bow shall be seen in the cloud.....and the waters shall no more become a flood to destroy all flesh."

The Greeks also dedicated this radiant flower to Juno, queen of heaven, who was held to be honoured mother of the gods, and was regarded as the symbol of light.

In more recent times, 1804, the English chemist, Tennant, when he discovered a new metallic element, which, on being dissolved in certain acids, produced a variety of colours, called it iridium, after the rainbow goddess, Iris.

Jasmine
Scattered Stars

Jasminum: (Oleacea)

Jasmine. Genus of deciduous or evergreen, woody-stemmed shrubs, scrambling or twining climbers, grown for their fragrant flowers and foliage. Jasmine.officianale or Common Jasmine can climb to 40 feet and has clusters of fragrant, 4-5 lobed, white flowers from summer – autumn. Some bear black berries after flowering. Jasmine was introduced to Europe in the mid 16th century and is widely grown for the perfume industry.

The exquisite beauty and perfume of the Jasmine has for centuries earned it the deserved devotion of many races, especially in relation to love. In India especially, Jasmine assumes a highly erotic significance and with Arab women Jasmine has a tradition as a nuptial flower. One species, Michelia.campaka, is a particular favourite with Hindu women who love wearing the golden stars of the campaka in their hair.

France, Italy, Morocco, Egypt, China, Japan and Turkey, grow Jasmine commercially to produce Oil for perfume. In France alone it is an industry worth over a billion dollars. Jasmine's sweet exotic oil is a deep orange-brown colour and her small white star shaped flowers are picked at night when the aroma is most intense.

One legend that relates to this night flower comes from Indian mythology and tells the story of a governor who once lived there who had a most lovely daughter. The sun became enamoured with the governor's daughter but shortly afterwards he deserted her for another. The unhappy maiden fell into such despair that she killed herself. A beautiful tree soon grew above her body, the flowers of which refused to open in the daytime. This night Jasmine's blossoms resemble those of the orange but have a more alluring perfume.

In Italy too, Jasmine is a bridal flower. According to legend there, in Tuscany, about 1699, the Grand Duke of Tuscany was given a beautiful gift of a variety of Jasmine named Goa jasione. This rare species had such beauty and fragrance that the Grand Duke jealously guarded it and strictly forbade his gardener to part with a single cutting. But the gardener was in love, and one day slipped one tiny perfumed spray into a posy he had made for his sweetheart. His girlfriend loved its perfume so much that she planted the little cutting into mulch in the hope it would grow and to her delight and surprise, it grew into a healthy plant.

Later, she raised more cuttings from the plant and sold them to enable her to marry her beloved gardener. In Tuscany thereafter, it was said "she who is worthy to wear the Jasmine wreath is worth a fortune to her husband."

Jasmine's origins probably lie in Iran although this wondrous plant has been cultivated in Asia and Europe since the 16th century for its perfume. Once flower syrups were made from Jasmine for coughs and leaf teas were used to rinse sore eyes and wounds. Jasmine flowers make a calming and sedative infusion taken to relieve tension. As well as its perfumery uses; the oil from Jasmine is considered antidepressant and relaxing. To herbalists, Jasmine's main properties are aromatic, anti-sposmatic, and expectorant.

One variety of Jasmine.sambac, Maid of Orleans, is the national flower of the Philippines – sampaguita. Sampaguita, a Spanish term, comes from the Phillipino words "sumpa kita" which means 'I promise you.' It is the promise of mutual love. In the early days, young people exchanged sampaguita garlands when marrying just like couples today exchange wedding rings. In the Philippines,
Jasmine is a symbol of purity, simplicity, humility and strength.

The same variety, Jasmine.sambac, is sacred to Vishnu and is used in Hindu ceremonies and is used for flavouring tea.

Though her roots are oriental, Jasmine has scattered her stars all over the world and being a strong and hardy plant grows well not just in tropical countries but is happy even in misty Scotland growing amongst the roses.

Lady Nairn of Scotland once wrote:-

The wild rose and the jessamine
Still hang upon' the wa,'
How mony cherished memories
Do they, sweet flowers, reca.'

Laurel
The Divine Crown of Greatness

Laurel: (Laurus Nobilis) and (Laurus azorica)

Laurel a dense, evergreen shrub with oval glossy, pointed leaves native to the Mediterranean regions. Clusters of small star-shaped, creamy yellow flowers with conspicuous stamens, appear in spring followed by dark purple berries. There are only two species of evergreen in this genus – Laurus Nobilis (bay, bay laurel, sweet bay) cultivated as a culinary herb, which occurs in southern Europe, the Canary Islands and the Azores, and Laurus azorica which is the Canary Island laurel. Laurus is from the Latin 'laus' meaning, "praise."

Love brought the Laurel into the limelight when the god Apollo fell in love with Daphne a mountain nymph.

He had been in love with her for a long time and once sought the death of a rival so that he could pursue her more vigorously. Apollo's rival, Leucippus, disguised himself as a girl so that he could join in with Daphne and the other nymphs' mountain revels. Apollo advised the mountain nymphs to bathe naked to ensure everyone in their company was a girl – Leucippus's imposture was discovered and the nymphs tore him to pieces.

Daphne was the daughter of the river god Peneius in Thessaly, and a priestess of Mother Earth, who, in the nick of time, spirited her away to Crete, and away from Apollo's advances.

In her place appeared the Laurel. Accepting his defeat, love-struck Apollo embraced the bush and with his power he bestowed on it the gift of evergreen-ness. To make sure that he would never forget his love, he resolved to wear perpetually a garland of Laurel leaves.

Apollo was also the god of poetry so thereafter, believing in Apollo's deep concern for those expressing beauty in verse, the Greeks honoured their poets by crowning them with the laurel wreath.
Since medieval times, to the present day, this practice of honouring great poets has continued in Britain where the monarchy appoints an official poet, referred to as the 'Poet Laureate,' in association with the ancient Greek tradition. The laureate's duties are to celebrate any occasion of national importance in poetry composed especially for the event. The first poet laureate was John Dryden who held office from 1668-88.

The laurel crown was also bestowed on winning athletes and leaders and in Roman times generals wore the laurel crown on their heads to symbolise victory. News of battle victories were often sent wrapped up in laurel leaves.

The bay leaves of the Laurel and her boughs were also prized for their magical properties. Prophets of the ancients used to hold laurel boughs when foretelling the future, and Laurel's bay leaves were eaten by the Pythian priestess before taking her seat in the sacred shrine at the Oracle of Delphi. The words spoken by the priestess were then reduced to verse and edited by the prophets.

Laurel's bay leaves were believed to protect people from sickness and in these old days many people planted a laurel tree near the house to protect its inhabitants from illness.

Leaves were also hung above the doors of the sick as a symbol of protection and this led to newly qualified doctors being garlanded with the laurel berry – bacca laureaus – which gave us the term baccalaureate, a University degree.

During thunderstorms, people observed that the Laurel was never struck by lightening and this encouraged their belief in the powers of Laurel" flowers, berries, leaves and boughs. To ward off negativity and evil, the ancients also wore
laurel bay leaves as an amulet. Leaves were placed under pillows to induce prophetic dreams – and to ensure that love will stay, couples would break a twig from the Laurel tree and keep one half each. Wishes, too, were once thought to come true if written on a bay leaf and then burned.

The Laurel is associated with glory, healing, physic powers, protection and strength. Today, her bay leaves are used by herbalists as a stimulant that improves digestion and locally as an antiseptic. They are also an important part of bouquet garni, commonly added to soups, sauces, stews and desserts.

Her golden garlands bring joy to our gardens and she truly is the food of love, Laurel.

Lavender
Sweet Aphrodisiac

Lavender: (Lavendula)

Is a small aromatic shrub, native mainly to Mediterranean regions and Atlantic islands, but grown all over Europe. Typical dry shrub; leaves narrow; sometimes deeply lobed, greyish, in opposite pairs; flowers two lipped, lavender or mauve, in dense spikes. It is widely cultivated for ornament and as the source for lavender oil for the perfume industry. (28 species; Family: Labiatae)

Lavender is amongst the most popular plants for herb gardens, having subtle colouring, and delightful fragrance. Producing the most pleasing of all garden scents, her beautiful, tiny blossoms send signals to many butterflies and bees as well as people.

In the Middle Ages, Lavender was thought to be the herb of love and was considered an aphrodisiac. Josephine Bonaparte thought so too, and to maintain Napoleon's sexual interest, Josephine would have a drink made from Lavender brought to him at night. This drink became Napoleon's favourite and it consisted of one part fresh coffee to three parts crunched up, fresh or dried, Lavender flowers. An equal amount of hot cocoa, made separately, would also be made and mixed with the above. (Alternatively, a thimble or so of cocoa liquor can be added.)

The ancient Egyptians loved Lavender too, and as well as using this herb in their mummification process, they used her fragrant oil to anoint sacred places.

Lavender gets her name from the Latin word, 'lavare,' which means 'to wash,' and the ancient Greeks, who bathed in water perfumed by Lavender, called the herb 'Nardus' which was an area of cultivation. In some old texts, Lavender is often called 'Spikenard.' The Greeks also enjoyed the therapeutic values of adding Lavender to their bathwater, just as we do today.

To freshen clothes, people in the old days often threw them over a bed of wild lavender, being aware too of Lavender's use as an insect repellent. It was the Romans, however, who brought this lovely plant to Britain. Essential to Julius Caesar's legions, they grew Lavender. Wherever they built bathhouses, they used Lavender oil in their baths. The soldiers also carried Lavender with them as an insect repellent and for medicinal uses.

Lavender is believed to promote calmness, tranquillity, to ease tension and depression, and to soothe tired muscles.

In the old day's, Lavender was used in spells to induce love, and prostitutes long ago wore its perfume to attract customers. Love letters were scented with Lavender and it was believed that the scent of Lavender placed under your pillow while making a wish before you fell asleep at night, would make your wish come true, if, you dreamed about the object of your wish whilst sleeping!

Lavender is not only prized for her beauty and perfume, but for her medicinal properties too. A flower or two added to tea can relieve headaches. In hot water, Lavender has a good, anti-bacterial affect. Scientific research has verified many of Lavender's ancient uses and her essential oils can be used on insect bites and burns and blemishes. As a cream, it helps eczema. As a lotion, it can be used for sunburn.

The flowers of Lavender are edible and can be crystallised in sugar for cake decoration. They can be used too as a flavouring.

Some of the uses old herbalists found for Lavender are interesting. According to one old herbal from the early 18th century, "it is good against the biting of serpents, mad dogs and other venomous creatures, being given inwardly and applied poultice-wise to the parts wounded." Lavender was also reputed to rid animals of lice and have a calming effect on lions and tigers!

Lavender is relatively pest free and can be used as an edging shrub, in containers, window boxes, or to keep pests away from her neighbours in your herb garden. Her flowers appear from June to August and for the best fragrance and oil, harvest them just as soon as they start opening.

With her glorious colours and enchanting perfume, Lavender has regained her throne as the Queen of Aromatherapy and every garden summer scented with her blossoms is a pleasure to our senses.

The Lily
Flower to the Sky Mother

Lily: (Lillium)

A perennial with a bulb formed from swollen, overlapping, scale like leaves, native to temperate regions, stem erect, unbranched with numerous narrow, alternate, or whorled leaves; flowers with six perianth - segments, large and often hanging, usually trumpeted with perianth rolled back. In a wide range of colours mostly white, yellow to red, purple, sometimes spotted, with long protruding stamens.

Prized for their beauty and often fragrant blooms, lilies are emblematic of light, purity, majesty and innocence, and are considered by some as the most beautiful flowers in the world.

The Greeks dedicated the Lily to Hera, the "skymother." One legend tells how, Jupiter wishing to render the infant Hermes immortal, caused Hypnos, the god of sleep, to prepare a narcotic which he persuaded Hera to drink. The sky mother fell into a deep sleep, and Jupiter laid the little Hermes in her arms so that he might drink the divine milk that would ensure immortality. The eager infant drew faster than he could swallow, and some of the escaping milk fell down to earth, there immediately sprung from it, the white Lily.

Another legend tells that the first Lillie's on Earth were not white but were all a lovely saffron hue, until sea born Aphrodite, appearing suddenly before them, whiter than the foam from which she springs, so bright, so delicate, caused the Lillie's to tremble by her perfect beauty, and waxing pale from jealousy, they lost their hue and blossomed white.

Signifying moral beauty and purity, the Lily was dedicated to the Virgin Mary by the early Christian church, hence the common name, "Lady Lily." As a heraldic emblem the Lily has played an important part. As early as 1048, the order of the Knights of St Mary of the Lily was instituted by Garcius, fourth King of Navarre, and in 1403, Ferdinand of Aragon also created an Order of the Lily, the collar of which was formed of Lillie's and gryphons.

The emblem of Florence is the white Lily, and the city of Dundee in Scotland carries Lillies on its arms. The water Lily is associated with July and according to the Victorian Language of the Flowers, represents – majesty with honour, and, pure of heart.

The Lily-of-the-Valley
Ladders to Heaven.

(Convallaria majalis)

A perennial growing to 20cm (Convallaria majalis), the lily-ofthe- valley is native to Europe and Asia; leaves elliptical, in pairs, the stalks sheathing, flowers dropping, globular bells with six short lobes, white, fragrant, berries red. It is cultivated for ornament, and as a source of perfume.

The Lily-of-the-Valley is the beautiful emblem of humility, of purity, and of unconscious sweetness. In the days of King Solomon, in the Song of Sons (2,1) it was used to express loveliness.

Indigenous to most European countries, the Lily-of-the- Valley grows freely in the woods of Norway, Sweden and Germany. In Britain it is not so frequently found in its wild state, but invariably to be found in gardens where no blossom shows fairer that this pale lily whose pure loveliness and sweetness cause it to be loved and admired.

The Germans have a particular affection for "little Maybells," as they call them, and at Whitsuntide, houses were made fragrant and beautiful by their deliciously sweet scenting blooms. French people know Lily-of-the-Valley as "Mary's tears."

In pagan times, the Lily-of-the-Valley was assigned to Ostara, Norse Goddess of day and of light. From her, it passed to the Virgin Mary, to whom, as emblematic of purity, it was dedicated by the monks and nuns of mediaeval days.

In some parts of England these beautiful lilies are still known by their old name of "May Flowers," and "May lillies," and the very lovely name of "ladders to heaven."

One legend tells how, in the forest of St. Leonard, the young warrior saint of that name met and faced with the mighty dragon Sin; how for three whole days and nights, single handed, the brave youth wrestled with the foe, until happily, the fourth day brought him victory, and saw the hideous dragon driven into the deep recesses of the world. Wherever St. Leonard's blood had stained the ground, there, every year, vale lilies spring and softly chime their bells to mark the victory won for God.

The sight of those beautiful, waxy, little bell flowers amidst the woodlands just cannot fail to bring happy surprise.

The Lotus
Dreamy Inspiration

The Lotus: (Nelumbo Necifera,) (Nymphaea) and (Zizyphus)

Lotus is the name given to three plants. The sacred lotus of India and China is Nelumbo Necifera, an aquatic perennial with thick rhizomes and glaucaus, it has peltate leaves up to 32" (80cm) in diameter. This Lotus has large fragrant pink or white flowers, followed by pepperpot receptacles containing hard nuts. In old Egypt, their favourite, the Nymphaea lotus, is a species of water lily and the lotus of classical Greek times is known as Zizyphus lotus, a type of jujube tree. The common lotus, a genus of the pea family, consists of about 100 species whose colours are yellow, white, red or purple and resemble the flowers of the pea family.

The outstandingly beautiful Lotus has been considered sacred since ancient times and antiquity has not reduced Lotus' venerable flame as she continues to inspire us just as she inspired those of earlier days.

Ancient Greek mythology tells of a race of people, thought to have lived in North Africa, whose only food was the classical type of Lotus. Known as the Lotophagi, it was said that this race of lotus-eaters ate both the fruit and the blossoms of the plant. The Greek epic poem, the Odyssey, describes an encounter between Odysseus and the lotus-eaters.

People who ate the magical plant forgot their homeland and the ties of friendship and family. Today people who daydream, or think of impractical ideas are sometimes called lotus-eaters! In Hindu legend, the sacred lotus, (Nelumbo Nucifera) was created from the Supreme Being's navel. Inside a golden lotus flower sat Brahma, who turned the Lotus into a New World. To these Hindu worshippers, the Lotus was a symbol of the solar matrix, the maternal womb from which the sun rose to renew the world.

According to the Buddhists, Buddha first appeared floating on a Lotus and is depicted on a lotus throne sitting in the position known as the 'lotus position.' For the gentle Buddha, the Lotus, with its large white bloom, was so outstanding in the muddy water that it symbolised the enlightened one. The White Lotus has been adopted as the official symbol of Buddhism and represents many things to Buddhists. In its closed position it represents potential, with eight petals it represents cosmic harmony, and a thousand petals showing means spiritual revelation.

The sacred lotus, (Nelumbo Nucifera) species, is Asian in origin and is sacred in Chinese, Tibetan and Indian cultures. Germinating in mud, this magnificent species unfolds its flowers in the sunlight and is seen as analogous to the growth of consciousness, purity and enlightenment. The sacred Lotus is the national flower of India.

The sacred Lotus occurs also in North America and from warm parts of Asia to Australia. Although native to Asia, it is grown world wide in tropical pools for its wonderful leaves and exquisitely beautiful flowers.

For the old Egyptians of 4,000 years ago, however, it was the Nymphaea Lotus that was held in high esteem. Revered as a symbol of the Nile, the Lotus was sacred to Isis, goddess of fertility, and was associated with the sun god, Ra. It appears symbolically in Egyptian architecture and paintings.

Around the world, Lotus symbolises; Purity, Resurrection, Evolution, Potential, Joy, Pure Affection; is said to be the "cradle of creative might," and known by some to "hold the secrets of the gods."
From East to West, the day dreamy Lotus seems to have inspired thoughts of divine goodness that have grown from seed to bud and bloom throughout the ages to many cultures, and long may she continue to do so!

Marigold
Golden Flower of the Greeks

Marigold: (Calendula officinalis)

Annual to perennial, growing to 27in., the Marigold is lightly sticky to the touch, leaves paddle shaped, flower heads up to 7cm., outer ray florets orange and yellow. Native to Southern Europe.

Once used for colouring butter, fabrics and cosmetics, this brilliant, yellow flower was also used by monks to make wounds heal faster.

Associated with May, formerly the Marigold was employed on May Day festivals in England in the formation of garlands for decking the May Queen, and in Germany too, was similarly employed, its blossoms garlanded the cow that led the procession!

In some parts of America, Marigolds were styled as "death flowers," in reference to a tradition that the crimson splashed species first sprang from the ground stained by the blood of the unfortunate Mexicans who fell victims to the love of gold and arrogant cruelty of the early Spanish settlers.

Emblematic of affection, sympathy and joy in sorrow, the Marigold was considered from its colour by the Greeks as the "golden flower."

The origin of the Marigold is unknown, though some say the flower first blossomed at the time of the Feast of the Annunciation, and was therefore dedicated to the Virgin Mary and named in her honour, and, in reference to its beautiful colour, became known as "Mary's Gold."

There is an old legend, however, that gives a more poetic origin to the name, and tells of a maiden who once lived, called Caltha, who became so in love with the sun that she sat all day long, eyes riveted upon the heavens, and at length refused to leave even at night, in case she missed the sun rise. And so she continued to gaze until the sun absorbed her in his rays and she vanished from mortal eyes. In her place appeared a flower, coloured like the sun, which had never been seen before, and at the closing of the day, with the departure of the sun god, she shut up her petals until touched by his rays in the morning of each new day. Married to the golden sun, her name was Marigold.

Today, a glistening presence in our gardens and loved just as ever, Marigold continues to impress.

Marjoram
Herb of Magic

Marjoram: (Origanum.vulare)

*Native to Europe, Asia and the Mediterranean. A bushy
perennial, Marjoram's leaves are oval. Bears clusters of small
two-lipped flowers, white or purplish-pink, daisy like, in dense
spikes. Grows up to 2 ft. Cultivated as a culinary herb often
named Oregano. Strongly aromatic. (Family: Labiatae)*

Marjoram, also known as Oregano, is one of the best
used of the seasoning herbs from our gardens. Oregano is
made from wild Marjoram's dried leaves and this plant is
a member of the mint family.

In old Greek and Roman times, Marjoram was used to
crown bridal couples with wreaths of Marjoram's daisy
like flowers to symbolise love and honour. The Greeks
also grazed their cattle on it believing that it would help
produce tastier meat. They then used the plant's leaves in
their dried form to flavour their meat, fish vegetables and
even wine. To these ancients, the name Oreganum meant
two things. The first part of the word, 'oreus' means 'of
the mountain' and the second 'ganos' means 'joy' so to
them, Oreganum meant 'Joy of the mountain.'

The goddess of love, Venus, according to the ancients, gifted Marjoram her aromatic fragrance and this led to a tradition they had that anointing oneself with it could cause dreams of a future spouse. The early Greeks also considered Marjoram to be a
herb of magic because they believed the original plant was created by the gods of Mount Olympus. The dried leaves, Oregano, were thought to hold mystical powers. They associated it with good luck, health, and carried it with them as a protection against poisons.

Marjoram's medicinal properties were also valued by the ancient Greeks. They used it as an aid to digestion, to allay anxiety, for convulsions and dropsy. For external injuries they made poultices from it. Chinese doctors have used Oregano for centuries and in Europe it is still used to improve digestion and soothe coughs.

In Italy, Marjoram is a favourite in the kitchen where it is used to flavour pizzas and spaghetti dishes. American soldiers brought Marjoram home from the Mediterranean after the second World War and most Oregano used in the USA is made from the leaves of wild Marjoram. Marjoram escaped from cultivation and grows wild in eastern North America.

Her lovely long stemmed flowers are great for cutting and can be dried for pot pourri. They can even be put in your bath for sweet smelling water. Easily grown, Marjoram will not only compliment your food, her loveliness with compliment your garden.

Narcissus
The Flower of the Poets!

Narcissus : (Amaryllidaceae)

*A bulb native to Europe, the Mediterranean region, and W.
Asia; strap shaped leaves; solitary flowers on a long stalk, central trumpet or
cup (the corona), surrounded by six "perianth" - segments, white, yellow, or
pink; the corona often contrasting. Horticulturally a division is made into
daffodils, and narcissi. Many species and numerous cultivars are grown in
gardens and in market gardens for florists.*

The name Narcissus is derived from the Greek word,
narke, signifying "torpor," in reference to the narcotic
properties of the plant. Homer states that, although the
Narcissus "delights heaven and earth by its beauty, yet at
the same time produces stupidity, madness and even
death."

One legend tells of Pluto, causing the flower to spring
up in order to lure beautiful Persephone from her home.
"A thing of marvellous blossom it was, and a glory to all
beholders, both immortal gods and mortal men." And as
she stoops to gather the fragrant bloom, the whole plain
quakes and trembles.
Suddenly from the earth rises Dis, seizes the terrified
Persephone, and places her in a waiting chariot, whose
coal black horses bear her away down into the gloomy
kingdom of which she became the queen.

In France, where the Narcissus is found in a wild state, with petals ethereal white, it is popularly known as Jeanetteblanche, and its yellow sister is known as Jenette-jaune.

The Narcissus was given to Venus, owning to its beauty and fragrance, and is noted as one of the blossoms in which the goddess bathed, in order to enhance her charms in the eyes of Paris, when competing with Juno and Diana for the golden apple, a prize of beauty.

According to Greek legend, the beautiful youth Nemises is responsible for the origin of Narcissus. Nemises so loved his own reflection in the stream, he slipped into the water and was drowned. When weeping Echo and her sister nymphs prepared the funeral urn for the beloved youth, they found his body missing. He was metamorphosed into a flower, Narcissus. Heartbroken Echo so loved Nemises, that she wasted away to a voice.

The narcissus poeticus, whose exquisite blooms were deemed worthy to crown the brows of the goddesses with stars, has always been a favourite of the poets, amongst them Keats and Shelley.

Nasturtium
The Bright Spark

Nasturtium: (Trapaeolum majus)

Is garden Nasturtium, a fast growing annual with almost circular leaves. Yellow to orange, long spurred slightly scented flowers appear from early summer followed by globuse fruits. Can climb up to 10 feet. A genus of over 90 species, native to
South America.

The garden Nasturtium's dazzling display of hot coloured flowers can brighten up the shadiest places producing an atmosphere of energy and light. So much so that some say the flowers of this plant, in the warm summer month, have been noticed to give out electric sparks at sunset!

Since it was brought back to Europe from Peru by the Spanish, this spectacular flowering climber has become a firm favourite of gardeners around the world, and is grown by many of them for culinary uses. All parts of the garden Nasturtium are edible. Hot and peppery, her leaves and flowers are a bright
addition to salads and freshly chopped, add flavour to egg and cheese dishes. Nasturtium's immature pods can be pickled and the mature nut like seeds can be roasted, and

used in pepper pots. During World War 2, Nasturtium seeds were used as a substitute for black pepper.

Nasturtiums' peppery taste was what gave it its first European name, Indian Cress. Trapaeolum comes from the Greek word 'tropaion' meaning 'trophy,' since garden Nasturtiums leaves are shaped like shields with helmet like flowers.

The original flower of garden Nasturtium, in her native land, was yellow, but breeding has produced different varieties of reds, orange and yellows. The Indians of Peru used the leaves for medicinal purposes to treat coughs, colds and 'flu. High in vitamin C, Nasturtiums act as a natural antibiotic and were also used as a poultice for cuts.

In Tolkien's 'Lord of the Rings,' the flowers in Bilbo's garden are called "Nasturtians." Tolkien insisted that his publishers leave the word in after consulting a gardener. To gardeners at that time, flowering Tropaeolum were 'Nasturtians' and the aquatic watercress (Nasturtium.officinale) was 'Nasturtium.'

Without garden Nasturtium in it, Monet's famous garden at Giveray would have been different. Monet let his Nasturtium grow into a glorious path instead of making them climb. To do this, sow plenty of seeds at the edges of both sides.

According to Feng Shui, Nasturtiums can be planted to harmonise the energies between buildings and land.

The sun brings out the spice in garden Nasturtium,

grown in the shade, her flavour is milder, but wherever you grow her fast growing seeds, this bright spark will lighten up your garden.

Poinsettia
The Very Beautiful Flame Leaf

Poinsettia: (Euphorbia pulcherrima)

A deciduous shrub native to Mexico. The flower is in fact a specialised inflorescence (cyathium) with large vermilion bracts resembling petals. (Family: Euphprbiaceae). Native to Mexico, there are over 100 varieties.

The brilliant Poinsettia's petal-like bracts are actually bright red leaves which surround her tiny greenish-yellow blossoms. The
Aztecs called her Cuetlaxochitle and used the plants bracts to make a reddish dye.

The USA' first ambassador to Mexico, Joel R. Poinsett, so admired this brilliant indigenous plant whilst he was there, that he sent specimens of it, in 1828, to the USA, where it soon flourished and was named Poinsettia by a horticulturist named
William Prescott.

Poinsettia's botanical name, Euphorbia pulcherrima, was given to the plant by a German botanist, named Wilenow after it grew through a crack in his greenhouse and amazed him with its beautiful colour. It means 'very beautiful.'

In her native Mexico, she also has a Spanish name, Flor de nochebuena, and Mexicans since the 18th century have associated Poinsettia with the Christmas season.

One Mexican legend about Poinsettia's origins tells of a child who sadly knelt before the altar at his village church on Christmas Eve. The poor child could not afford to get a gift to offer the Christ Child on his birthday. His sincerity brought about a miracle and the first "flower of the Holy Night" bloomed at his feet.

Another legend tells a similar story, again from Mexico, only this time a little girl, on her way to church, weeps because she has no gift to offer the Christ Child. Through her tears, an angel appeared and instructed her to gather weeds and take them to church. When the little girl arrived at the altar with her wilting offering, starry crimson blossoms burst forth from every stem. Poinsettia became symbolic of the star of Bethlehem and it is traditional in Mexico to give Poinsettia plants at Christmas.

As Poinsettia has spread her roots over the Americas, she has gained many lovely names. To Chile and Peru, she is the Crown of the Andes and Lobster Flower since her leaves come in pink and white as well as vibrant red. In Central America she is also known as the Flame Leaf Flower. In the USA, Poinsettia has become so popular that ninety percent of all Poinsettias are exported from there today.

On family from the USA have become a legend in their own time owing to Poinsettia. The Ecke family of

California began growing this wonderful plant in the early 1900's outdoors for use as landscape plants and as cut flowers. Eventually, they grew them in greenhouses too and are now the leading producers of Poinsettia in a business that makes over 220 million dollars during the Christmas holiday season. December 12th is National Poinsettia Day in the USA.

The giving of the very beautiful flame leaf, Poinsettia, has evolved from a tradition adopted in her indigenous home in Mexico to many other parts of the world. This brilliant gift from Mexico truly symbolises the spirit of Christmas.

The Poppy
Summer's Kiss

The Poppy: (Papaveraceae)

*Poppy is the name given to members of the family
Papaveraceae. All produce latex, are often brightly coloured, and have flowers
with two sepals and four overlapping petals, often crumpled when they first
open.*

The Poppy of the cornfields was held by the ancients
to be favourable to the growth of corn, and was dedicated
to Ceres, goddess of harvests, who is usually represented
as adorned with wheat-ears and poppy flowers.

With the Greeks, the number of seeds in the Poppy
symbolized, generation, and Venus was sometimes
represented as holding in one hand an apple and in the
other a Poppy flower. But it was to Diana, queen and
huntress, that the field Poppy, growing where no step had
trod, uncontaminated by man, more especially belonged.

Young Greek girls would test the fidelity of their
lovers by placing in the palm of the hand a Poppy petal,
which, if when sharply struck responded by a loud crack,
signified sincerity, but which, if it broke, signified
unfaithfulness. From Greece, this love test spread
throughout other parts of Europe. In some parts of

Holland and Germany, so traditional have the prophetic powers of the Poppy become, that it is known as the "cracking rose" or "confession rose."

Popig, the old Saxon name for Poppy, is thought to have been given because of the practice of mixing the seeds of the common scarlet species with the food of infants to induce sleep, and it is in its character of sleep that the Poppy has become famous.

The true opium Poppy has, however, always white blooms, with a large purple stain at the base of the petals. This is the renowned "drowsy poppy" from the capsules of which opium has been prepared for over twenty five centuries.

According to one Bengali legend, these narcotic properties were the result of a rashi or magicians spell. The rashi, who lived on the bank of the River Ganges, had given a mouse the power of speech, and then transformed it into a cat, a dog, an ape, a boar, and then later transformed it into a beautiful maiden to whom he gave the name Postomani, or Poppy seed lady. Postomani deceived the king into believing she was of royal blood and he married her.

After a time of happiness together, the couple were separated by Postomani's untimely death. The rashi, attempting to console the king, revealed the deception and told the king of her true origin saying, "Let her body remain in the well, fill up the well with earth and out of the flesh and bones will grow a plant which shall be called Posto - the Poppy tree. From this plant will be obtained a drug called opium, which will either be smoked or swallowed as a wondrous narcotic till the end of time. If abused, it will generate the consumer one quality of each of the animals to which Postomani has been transformed. He will be mischievous like a mouse, fond of milk like a cat, quarrelsome like a dog, filthy like an ape, savage like a boar, high tempered like a queen."

Red Poppies which grew wild in the fields of Flanders in France are used as a symbol of remembrance of those who died in the two World Wars.

This delicately petalled bloom is also known as Summer's kiss. Francis Thompson (1859-1907) wrote:-

"Summer set lip to earth's bosom bare,
And left the flushed print in a poppy."

Primrose
The Lady of Spring !

Primrose: (Primula vulgaris)

A stemless perennial native to Europe, W. Asia and N. Africa, a rosette of crinkled, tongue-shaped leaves, flowers long-stalked with a tubular calyx and spreading, pale yellow, rarely pink petals. A plant of woods and hedges, it is decreasing in numbers because of excessive destruction of woodlands and picking. The garden polyanthus is derived from a hybrid with the cowslip.

Associated with February, the Primrose cheers and consoles after the long winter, provoking simple happiness. Despite its unassuming look, the humble Primrose is a heraldic flower, giving name to a noble Scottish house whose motto is:

"Early youth is charming"
"Fair fragile lovely thing
Firstling of a happy Spring"

At one time, the Primrose was a bridal flower, and was also used by young girls to test the truth or trustworthiness of a lover, and young men used it once as a love token, sending it bespearled with dew.

Owing to the close botanical connection with the cowslip, the Primrose is fabled to have once been a beautiful youth called Paralisos, son of the Goddess Flora, who, being parted from his beloved nymph, pined away and died, and was changed by his mother into a flower.

Known of old as "The Lady of Spring," the pale Primrose was regarded not only as the emblem of early youth, but of shadowed love, which may be accounted to its use as a funeral flower. Shakespeare confirms this in "Cymbeline," where Arviragus, believing Imogen(Fidele), to be dead, declares that while summer lasts, he will sweeten her sad grave with fairest flowers:
"Thou shalt not lack
The flower, that's like thy face, pale primrose;"

In the legend of St Orian, the primrose has place among the flowers that bloom in Paradise.

Also known as sister to the violet, these two beauties compliment the bride as well as each other when set together in the bridal posy. The Primrose, although associated with February, can be seen gracing our woodlands and gardens as late as May.

The Rose
Aphrodite's Favourite Blossom

Rose: (Rosaceae)

Genus of deciduous or semi-evergreen open shrubs and scrambling climbers, grown for their profusion of fragrant flowers, and sometimes for their fruits,(rose hips); leaves are divided into usually 5 or 7 oval leaflets with round or pointed tips, sometimes toothed. Stems usually bear thorns or prickles. Fully hardy, prefer open, sunny sites. Flowers occur in a variety of forms, single, semi-double, or fully double. Wild species usually produces a single flower (4-7 petals), mainly in summer followed by red or black hips in autumn.

Prized for centuries for their beauty and as a source of perfume, roses are probably the world's most widely cultivated ornamental plants. Many traditions tell of the first Rose. The Arabs believed the first Rose to have sprung from a drop of sweat from the brow of Mohamet.

In Christian tradition, the original Rose grew in the Garden of Eden. It had no thorns. A flower of pure beauty, it gave only pleasure and never hurt. The thorns were added after man's fall.

The Persian poets tell us that the first Rose bloomed in Gulistan at the time the flowers demanded from Allah a new sovereign, because the drowsy lotus would slumber at night.

The old Greeks, fabled the Rose to have once been a nymph, who, roused from sleep by a kiss from Apollo, transformed herself into the flower. For the Greeks, the Rose symbolized love, and beauty and they dedicated it to Aphrodite.

One legend tells how, at first the beautiful Rose was snowy white, until the nightingale, falling into such ecstasy of love over her charms, and disregarding the thorns that tore his breast, pressed his beating heart against her soft petals, and from the crimson flood of his wounds, he dyed her white bosom red.

As a heaven sent flower, the Rose is the most frequently mentioned flower in legends of the saints. One of these tells how a maiden, unjustly accused of wrong doing, was condemned to be burned to death. As the flames were about to be lit, she called to God to deliver her and make her innocence clear to all men.

As soon as the flames leapt around her, they were suddenly extinguished, the wood turning into freshly sprouting Rose bushes. Those pieces not yet alight, showing pure white blooms, those already kindled glowing with crimson blooms. Since then the Rose has been the emblem of Christian martyrdom.

The stories of the Rose, both romantic, and mystical, must number in the thousands, yet the Rose retains the secret of her mysterious origin, just like love! No wonder this flower is the flower of St.
Valentine's Day.

Rosemary
Dew of the Sea

Rosemary: (Rosmarinus officinalis)

An evergreen shrub native to Southern Europe, bears shiny, dark green leaves and small, pale blue flowers. Grows wild in the Mediterranean region and measures from 2 – 6 feet (60-180 cms. High). (Family: Lamiaceae – mint family)

For centuries throughout Europe, pretty Rosemary has been associated with remembrance and her reputation has spread as far as Australia today where a sprig of Rosemary is worn on Anzac Day in memory of the dead.

Today, Rosemary is regarded as "Mary's shrub" in honour of the Virgin, but the official name of this herb, Rosmarinus, given to her by the old Greeks, means "dew of the sea" and indicates an association with Aphrodite the sea goddess, and an old Greek goddess, the Titan Mnemosyne (Memory.) This memory goddess, met her worshippers at a dark pool and took back from them all the memories she permitted them in life so that they would not suffer when they past over. The goddess of memory was thought by the ancients to be a loving and beautiful queen of darkness. Therefore, Rosemary, in ancient Greece and Rome, was associated with love, remembrance and death where its use in marriage and funeral rites signified enduring affection. Loving couples, about to be married, had Rosemary entwined into their head dresses to help them remember their wedding vows and Greek students wore sprigs of this lovely fragrant herb in their hair to help their memory during examinations.

The old ancients of Egypt placed Rosemary in tombs to remember their loved ones and used the herb in embalming, and later Egyptians told an old myth associating Rosemary with Mary and Egypt, in relation to the colour of Rosemary's blossoms. The story says, that when Mary and Joseph fled to Egypt with the Holy Child, Mary laid her cloak on a Rosemary bush and from that moment Rosemary's flowers became blue.

From Sicily too, comes a legend explaining why Rosemary's blossoms are blue. An old goddess, Circe, who caused violent volcanoes to erupt and plants to wither and die, once enchanted the inhabitants of Sicily so that they would throw themselves into the sea. One beautiful blue-eyed woman who held on to the cliffs was transformed into a Rosemary bush
to remind men of the ever-renewing power of good.

Folklore surrounding Rosemary shows that this plant's fragrant herbal properties were important to people in the past and Rosemary played a part in many festivals, customs and belief. People put Rosemary under their pillows to prevent nightmares and it was once thought someone could be made to fall in love by simply being touched on the finger with a sprig of this divine herb.

Sixteenth century Europeans carried Rosemary in

pouches to ward off the plague and judges placed it on their benches to protect them from typhoid.

Her narrow leaves are used as a culinary herb, in aromatherapy and in baking and pouches of dried Rosemary leaves have also been used as an insect repellent and to brew tea for headaches. Oil from Rosemary is said to have antibacterial and antifungal properties.

Rosemary has been associated with remembrance for thousands of years and Shakespeare's Ophelia confirms a continuing tradition where, in Hamlet, she states 'There's a Rosemary for remembrance.' As does the Victorian 'Language of Flowers.'

From the earliest of times, whether she's growing in our gardens or growing wild, the beautiful sight of masses of blossoming Rosemary, like a hazy blue mist from the sea, cannot fail to stir the heart. Who could forget Rosemary?

The Shamrock
Symbol of Hope!

The Shamrock: (trifolium)

*Native to Europe, N. Africa, and the W. African islands
(Macaronesiea), Shamrock or trifolium is the name applied to plants with
leaves divided into three leaflets, including wood sorrel and various species of
clover. A slender annual growing to 10," flowers yellow, up to 15 clustered in
tiny stalked heads. Petals later turning dark brown.*

According to Celtic legend, when St. Patrick landed at
Wicklow in A.D. 433, he had difficulty explaining to the
people of Ireland that Got was a sacred spirit, who
created heaven and earth, and that the Trinity is
contained in Unity. To illustrate his meaning, he plucked
a Shamrock from the grass and cried:

"Is it not possible for the Father, Son, and the Holy
Ghost to be One, as for these three leaves to grow
together on a single stalk?" Hence the name old name for
the Shamrock, herba Trinitatis.

The word Shamrock is related to seamrog, which
appears to be generic, being applied to many clovers, the
black medick, the pimpernel and the wood sorrel, each

one which has been claimed to have been the original Shamrock

For the old Greeks and Romans, it was a magic plant protecting against snakes and scorpion stings. Regarded as highly sacred, it was largely employed in their religious rites and ceremonies.

The grass crown composed of Shamrock leaves and was esteemed a mark of high honour. Spes, or Hope, was a beautiful child standing on tip-toe, a shamrock in her hand, and for the Irish too, the "immortal shamrock," or St. Patrick's cross, is an emblem of hope.

The Druids held the Shamrock in great esteem, because its leaf symbolized the three departments of nature - sea, earth, and heaven.

As a "holy herb" the Shamrock was considered disgusting to witches, and protected against all evil, worn alike by peasant and knight as a potent charm.
Pliny states that serpents are never seen upon the Shamrock and according to legend, St. Patrick drove all reptiles from the Emerald Isle.

On St Patrick's day, 17th March, children had Shamrocks pinned to their sleeves, and when the social cup was pledged the ceremony of drowning the Shamrock was duly observed:

*"For show me the true hearted son of old Erin,
Who loves not the land where the green Shamrock grows."*

Snowdrop
A Snow Piercer!

Snowdrop: (Gilanthus nivalus)

A bulb sometimes flowering in late winter, native to Europe and W. Asia, strap shaped leaves, bluish green with flowers on long stalks, solitary, drooping, white, three outer segments spreading, three inner smaller, with green spot at base of apical notch.(Gilanthus nivalus)

Associated with January, the Snowdrop is thought to have been introduced to Britain during the reign of Queen Elizabeth.

The Snowdrop is regarded as the emblem of *promise* and *consolation*. Pushing it's way through the cold, hard soil of Winter, blooming whiter than the snow, the Snowdrop heralds Spring's imminent arrival. Wherever this little token grows, all are cheered by the sight of those welcome little bells.

The French know it as "snow piercer" or "winter's wooer." In Italy, it is the "firstling" and in some parts of Switzerland, the people call it the "blackbird flower" because with the appearance of these little blossoms, the blackbird begins to sing.

In Germany, where it has long since been a sacred and cherished flower, it signifies youthful love, and simplicity. They call it the "little snow bell."
The Spaniards give it a similar name, "little white bell," whilst in Wales, it is known fondly as "baby bell."

One legend tells how, once, Hope was bent and weeping above the white snowy blanket of Earth, mourning the flowers and all the lovely green things buried beneath the cold, hard soil when, suddenly, where her tears dropped upon the frozen snow, it melted, and Snowdrops graced the ground revealed, the messengers of her comfort.

Another legend, of German origin, states: When, at the Creation, all things were coloured, the heavens blue, the clouds grey, the earth brown, the flowers, all hues, the snow approached the Lord God and complained that for him no colour remained, and that therefore he would be as little noticed as the wind. The Creator bade him go to the flowers and ask from them a colour.

But no flower would share with the snow her brilliant hue. Snow, giving up, was about to turn away, when the humble Snowdrop murmured, "If my white colour be of any use to you, you are very welcome to it." And since that time, the snow guards and keeps warm, the generous little flower.

To some, the Snowdrop is a sign of *hope, friendship and adversity*. Some too, see the Snowdrop as a symbol of *purity, of innocence, and humility.*

The little flower is said to have appeared when Mary took little Jesus to the Temple of Jerusalem, and was afterwards, held sacred to all virgins.

Burn's writes…
"Love's first virgin Snowdrop kiss."

The Spring Crocus
Morning Star

The Spring Crocus: (Iridaceae)

*A perennial producing corms, indigenous to North Africa,
North and Western Asia, and Southern Europe, not known in
Britain before the later part of the sixth century; leaves grasslike with distinctive
silvery stripe down centre; stalkless flowers, goblet-shaped with long, slender
tube, mainly white, yellow, or purple, closing up at night, many cultivated for
ornament.*

Save the brave pearled snowdrop, no flower is more
eagerly awaited, or more fondly welcomed than the
cheerful Crocus smiling up to heaven.

Emblematic of impatience and of youthful gladness,
and because it pushes its way through the cold, hard
ground of Winter, the Crocus signifies hope and
friendship in adversity.

The autumn flowering species produce flowers before
the leaves appear in the spring. Strangely, they are often
attacked by the birds, which prefer the
yellow flowers, no-one knows the reason.

The colourful Crocus, (from the Greek kroke,)is
known to have been employed by the ancients in the
formation of their floral crowns. Classic tradition fables

the Crocus to have sprung up on the spot where on occasion the mighty Jove reclined.

According to another legend, the Crocus is named among the flowers that helped to form the couch of Zeus and Hera when resting upon the summit of Mount Ida.

And one legend tells of how, when Venus attired herself in floral gown to win the prize of beauty, the Crocus was among the flowers, "with scent of which was Aphrodite clad;" while another states that, when the three goddesses came to the judgement of Paris, "at their feet the Crocus broke like fire."

Another flower of St.Valentine, and a favourite for planting in special remembrance, this lovely flower is a beautiful emblem of hope and everlasting life. This "morning star of all flowers" truly welcomes Spring.

Sunflower
Flower of the Sun Worshippers

Sunflower: (Helianthus. Annus)

Grown for their large, daisy-like heads, Sunflower or
Helianthus is a fast growing annual with bright, golden yellow leaves, which can
be oval to heart shaped. Its centre can be brown, purplish or black. There are
over 150 species of Sunflower. Some varieties are cultivated for their edible and
rich oil yielding seeds. Tall, intermediate, and dwarf cultivars are available,
some growing as tall as fifteen feet, (Helianthus. Annus), others only two or
three feet. (Family; Compositae).

The wonderful Sunflower, often the first seed grown by little children, is a world favourite. Originally growing in North America around 3000 BC, early explorers brought her to Europe in the 1500's where her popularity spread to Russia, the
Far East and Egypt.

Her golden beauty makes us smile and fills us with warmth, just like the sun, but it was for her usefulness and nourishing qualities that she was, and still is, prized. Many countries grow Sunflower for the seeds and oil her flowers produce. Every mature flower yields forty per cent of its weight as oil, and just one Sunflower head can produce up to one thousand seeds.

Her official name, Helianthus, comes from the Greek word 'Helios,' which means 'Sun,' and 'anthus,' which means flower.

Helios, according to Greek mythology, was the Sun and god of the Sun. His sisters were Selene, the Moon, and Eos, the dawn. Helios drove a four-horse chariot across the sky each day. Each evening, a huge golden cup brought him back to his palace in the east, on the river Oceanus. His daily journeys made him an all-seeing god and Greeks often called upon him to witness their oaths. The Island of Rhodes was sacred those who worshipped Helios and a famous statue of him once stood in the harbour there. One of the ancient wonders, it was known as The Colossus of Rhodes.

One Greek legend tells of Clytie, a nymph who fell in love with Helios. Helios scorned her in favour of the daughter of King Orchamus of Persia. Clytie was so jealous she told the King of his daughter's affair and he buried his daughter alive! This made Helios hate Clytie and she wasted away and became
the Sunflower, destined to follow the sun with her head forever as he journeys across the sky.

The old Incas too, worshipped the Sun and the Inca Emperor was said to be a direct descendant of the sun god Inti.
Incan priestesses wore large sunflower discs made of gold on their garments. In the 11th century, the Incas established their capital at Cuzco, the Sacred City of the Sun, where they built temples and fortresses, which they covered in sheets of gold.
The Spanish conquistador, Francis Pizarro, who

invaded the Inca Empire in the early 16th century, reported seeing the native Incas worshipping a giant Sunflower.

In the Andes Mountains, golden images of sunflowers were found in the temples there.
Central and North American natives used Sunflowers to make oil and for food, medicine and dye, and in the prairies of North America, the natives placed bowls of Sunflower seeds on the graves of their dead.

The Sunflower means many things to many people around the world. Before its break up, the Soviet Union produced more Sunflower seeds than any other nation and Kansas U.S.A. is known as the Sunflower State.

To the Chinese, the Sunflower symbolises longevity, to others; she represents nourishment, warmth, deep loyalty and constancy. In 1996, she became the symbol of a world free of nuclear weapons when, at a ceremony held on a former
Ukrainian missile base, Sunflowers were planted and their seeds scattered, after the Ukraine gave up its last nuclear warhead.

The poets too, have written of sunny Sunflower. Thomas Hood mentions the legend of Clytie in his poem 'Flowers.' But for Thomas Moore, the Sunflower was more than the flower of the sun worshippers, she meant true love
everlasting; -

> *No, the heart that has truly loved never forgets,*
> *But as truly loves on to the close,*
> *As the sun-flower turns on her god, when he sets,*

The same look which she turned when he rose.

Thomas Moore (1779-1852)
'Believe me, if all those endearing young charms' (1807)

Sweet Basil
Little Love

Sweet Basil: (Ocimum basilicum)

Erect, much branched aromatic with ovate bright green leaves up to 5cm (2in) long. Whorls of white, tubular flowers are borne from summer to mid-autumn. Over 100 species belong in this genus. Sweet Basil occurs most in warm and tropical regions, especially Africa.

The wonderful Sweet Basil is an aromatic plant of the mint family, the leaves of which are used as a culinary herb.

Recorded from the late Middle English, the name comes from Old French and Medieval Latin from the Greek *'basilikos'* 'royal.' In Latin, the name was confused with basiliscus, on the supposition that the plant was an antidote to the poison of a Basilisk – the mythical reptile with the lethal gaze or breath, which was hatched by a serpent from a cock's egg.

Native to India, the Sweet Basil of our gardens is sacred to the Hindu god Vishnu, whose wife Lakshmi was transformed into the herb. When a sprig of this divine plant is broken, the heart of Vishnu is said to be profoundly agitated. By Hindus, Sweet Basil is regarded as a protective plant and as a beneficent spirit that may open the gates of heaven. Therefore, when a Hindu dies, a leaf of Sweet Basil is placed upon his breast to ensure his safe passage to Paradise.

The old Greeks however, thought Sweet Basil a sinister plant, symbolising hatred and misfortune. They represented poverty by the figure of a female clad in rags seated by a plant of Basil.

According to legend, Alexander the Great sent it back to Greece not long before his death, and because of this, and the riots that broke out after his death, it was known to them as the devil's plant.

Yet, according to an old Moldavian legend, Sweet Basil is an enchanted herb whose spell can make a youth love the maiden from whose hand he accepts a sprig.

In Italy too, Sweet Basil bears a romantic character. In Tuscany, it is popularly known as "amorino," or "little love," and when removed by a maiden from her window, signifies to her lover that he is expected.

But the most famous legend from Italy in relation to Sweet Basil must be the touching Sicilian story of Isabella of Messina. Isabella's lover, Lorenzo, was killed by her own brothers. One night, Lorenzo's ghost appeared to her and told her where she could find his body. When she found it, poor Isabella wrapped up Lorenzo's head in linen and buried it in a
great pot beneath a plant of Sweet Basil to conceal it from her brothers.

Tended with love and care, and watered by her

heartbroken tears, the plant grew strong and filled Isabella's room with sweetness. Her brothers however, became so concerned about the time Isabella was spending alone in her room tending to her plant, that they took it away from her. Isabella cried unceasingly for its return. The brothers split the pot in order to find out what their sister was concealing and when they found the mouldering head, they recognised it as Lorenzo's.

Realising that the murder had been discovered, they buried it and fled to Naples. Isabella died of a broken heart.

Isabella's story inspired Keats to write:-

And she forgot the stars, the moon, and sun,
And she forgot the blue above the trees,
And she forgot the dells where waters run,
And she forgot the chilly Autumn breeze;
She had no knowledge when the day was done,
And the new moon she saw not: but in peace
Hung over her sweet Basil evermore,
And moistened it with tears unto the core.

'Isabella' or 'The Pot of Basil' (1820) st.53 John Keats.
In the West Indies, Sweet Basil is soaked in water and scattered around shops to attract buyers and for good luck.

Pots of Sweet Basil can often be found in the windows of Cretan country houses, where a small species of basil, the bush basil, is known in Crete as "love washed by tears."

The scent of Sweet Basil is also known to cause sympathy between two people and it is often added to love incenses and sachets. Fresh Basil leaves are rubbed against the skin as a natural love perfume.

According to some beliefs, sprinkling Basil powder over the heart of the one you love, whilst asleep, will ensure they remain true to you.

A popular culinary herb, indeed, a vital ingredient in Pizza and many other Italian dishes, Basil's sweet leaves are equally wonderful in all egg, cheese and vegetable dishes. They can be used in teas and herb breads and are used to flavour vinegar.

Wherever Sweet Basil grows and whatever its use, this wonderful versatile plant and her tiny white blooms can provoke our senses, which then, awakened, bring pleasurable experiences to us.

Sweet Peas
The Seeds of Life

Sweet Pea (Lathyrus.odoratus)

*Moderately fast growing, annual, tendril climber. Up to 10ft.
Fully hardy. Has oval, mid-green leaves with tendrils. Scented
flowers are produced in shades of blue, purple, pink or white from summer to
autumn. Native to Crete, Sicily and Southern Italy. Generally found in
northern temperate regions, tropical east African mountains and South
America.*

Grown for its wonderfully scented and colourful blossoms, Sweet Pea happily grows in a range of habitats, including sunny, sandy or shingle banks, grassy slopes and even open woodland.

Lathyrus.oderatus is the most widely grown of the many species available but it was not the first. The first, Lathyrus.sativus, was cultivated in the early Neolithic period and was perhaps even the first domesticated crop in Europe. The name Lathyrus comes from the Greek meaning 'pea' or 'pulse' and oderatus means 'fragrant'; and this plant is grown simply for its beauty and fragrance since it cannot be eaten.

A Franciscan monk, Father Francis Cupani, introduced it to wider cultivation in the 17th century after finding it growing in Sicily. He sent some seeds from it to a teacher, Dr. Robert Uvedale, in England in 1699.

Sweet Pea's popularity grew slowly at first in the UK, in 1800 there were only about five varieties, but in 1900, there were at least 264 varieties exhibited at the Crystal Palace in London. During that period, an Austrian Monk, Gregor Johann Mendel, experimented with the growing of Sweet Peas in the
Augustine monastery where he lived, and he made a monumental discovery. Through his painstaking research and mathematical calculations, he showed the principles of heredity, demonstrating how characteristics of parents of cross-bred offspring re-appeared in certain proportions of future generations.

When he tried to let others know about this marvelous discovery, no-one took notice of him, even though he published his findings in 1865. When he died in 1884, his work was not recognised. Then, in 1900, his history making theory was rediscovered
and received the worldwide recognition it deserved. Mendel's Law became the fundamental principle of the laws of heredity and today Mendel is known as the founding father of modern genetics because of the work he did breeding his Sweet Peas.

In 1901, another breeder, Silas Cole, who was Head Gardener to Earl Spencer of Althorp, produced a new hybrid Sweet Pea that caused a sensation. This Sweet Pea's frilly large blossoms outshone all the smaller cultivars. It was called 'Countess Spencer' and was the first of the Spencer hybrids of Lathyrus.oderatus. Most of the Sweet Peas grown today come from these hybrids.

In Edwardian times, Sweet Peas were considered to be the floral emblem of England and played an important part in the floral arrangements for every wedding or special occasion.

According to mythology, Sweet Peas sown before sunrise on St. Patrick's day will have more fragrant and larger blossoms, and this tradition has spread to other saint's days.

Whenever we choose to plant our Sweet Peas, we can be sure of one thing, whether they're tumbling from our baskets or climbing up our fences, Sweet Peas will colour our gardens with brilliance scented with sensory delight.

Sweet Violet
The Perfume of Venus

Sweet Violet: (Viola oderata)

A species of violet, lacking stems but with creeping stolons, native to Europe, Asia Minor, and North Africa. Its strongly scented flowers are distilled for perfume and for flavourings. However the scent quickly becomes mild because of the dulling effect of the chemical iodine.

Associated with February and March, from early times the Sweet Violet has been the chosen flower of romance, of *poetry, of chivalry and of love.* The purple variety is the emblem of *loyalty and of faithful love,* while the white variety is commonly regarded as the type of *candour, simplicity and innocence.*

The violet is found in nearly all parts of the world. In Persia of old, it ranked with the rose, and throughout the East is highly esteemed. With the ancients it was a flower of honour. It was the proud crown of Athenians. Said to be used by Venus as a perfume to win from Paris the prize of beauty, the Sweet Violet seems to have found favour everywhere.

Several classic legends account for the origin of the violet. One of these relates to how Ianthea, brightest of Diana's nymphs, was changed by the Goddess into a violet to save her from the wiles of the sun god.

According to one tradition, the violets were all white at first, until one day Venus, envious of Cupid's admiration of their purity and sweetness, turned them blue.

A Saxon legend tells how once, Czernebogh, God of Vandals, lived in a stately castle and how, when Christianity swept over Saxony, the god and his castle were turned into rocks, while his lovely young daughter was changed into a violet. Now this violet only blossoms once in a hundred years, and whoever plucks the flower will win the maiden and all her vast wealth.

Modesty, sweetness, humility, loyalty, content, these and more, are the attributes of the violet that made it the chosen emblem of Napoleon the First and Friedrich the First of Germany.

The violet was favoured as a bridal flower in the early days to enhance the posy of bridegrooms.
Blooming again in the Autumn, the Sweet Violet is a double joy.

The Scots Thistle
Husband to the Rose

The Scots Thistle: (Family: Compositae, Cirsium, Carduus)

*The name applied to several spiny plants of the daisy family,
Compositae, many belonging to genera Cirsium and Carduus.
All have leaves with spiny margins, often globular flower heads, overlapped by
spine-tipped bracts; florets reddish, purple, or white; the national emblem of
Scotland.*

Legend associates the Thistle with the Sicilian shepherd, Daphnis. Educated by the nymphs, inspired by the poetic muse, taught by Pan himself to play upon the pipe, this gifted youth was endowed by Diana with a passionate love of the chase. At his death, five of his favourite dogs pined away and died, while Earth, to mark the sadness of her grief, sent forth the first thorn and thistle.

According to Nordic tradition, the Thistle is a lightning plant, and was dedicated by the old Norsemen to Thor, god of war and thunder, hence, the thistle protects from all things evil.

The word thistle is akin to the Old Saxon - pistel, and the Dutch and German - Distel, the word being essentially the same in all Teutonic languages.

According to one legend, Hungarian, the oak has once asked in marriage the daughter of the thistle since, "the softest leaves that enfold the silk in the sweetest flower in the garden - are not softer than those that sting, not if you, but tenderly, touch them."

Dear to the Scots above all flowers, "saving the rose, and he is the rose's husband," the Thistle, with its bold motto, Nemo me impune lacessit, or, "Wha daur meddle wi' me," is the time honoured symbol of Scotland.

Before a decision was taken in the middle of the sixteenth century, in favour of the placing of the thistle on all banners in Scotland, the Thistle was exclusively the badge of Stuart. The Order of the Thistle claims to be the most ancient of all orders of honour, tradition holding it to have been instituted by Archius, King of Scots, when he was victorious in battle over Athelstan, born A.D.895, the grandson of Alfred the Great.

In fact, it is more recent an institution, for although James V had a collar of golden thistles, the Order of the Thistles was not instituted until the reign of James VII. The collar of the order is gold, with thistles and sprigs of rue interlaced and enamelled green, being the two ancient symbols of the Picts and Scots.

Ancient legend takes us back to the days of the Picts, in the time of Malcolm I, when a party of invading Danes attempted to invade Scotland and decided to attack at night. Noiselessly, under cover of darkness, they crept towards the slumbering camp, when suddenly one of their soldiers trod with his naked foot upon a thistle, as did the rest of them, so rousing the slumbering warriors who flew to arms and drove away the foe.

Marianus, the milk thistle, derives its name from the Virgin Mary, and was known in early days as "Our Lady's Thistle," a title which it likewise bears in France and Germany. It was also commonly known as the "holy thistle" and the "blessed thistle."
An Order of the Thistle was instituted in France in A.D. 1370, in honour of the Virgin Mary.

The guardian Thistle is regarded as the symbol of independence and of retaliation.

The Tulip
Sister to the Star of Bethlehem

The Tulip! (Liliaceae)

*A bulb native to Europe and Asia, stems erect, leaves narrow to oval,
sometimes wavy; flowers solitary, in a variety of shapes and colours with six
rounded or pointed and sometimes fringed,
perianth - segments or tepals. Genus: Tulipa, 100 species, Family: Liliaceae.*

To the Eastern people of old, the Tulip was highly
esteemed, especially in Syria where it grows in such
abundance, it is often called "lily of the field," and is the
symbol of passionate consuming love.

According to classic legend, the Tulip was once a
beautiful Dalmatian nymph, who was endowed by her sea
god father with his love of bright changing colours. One
day Vertumnus, god of Spring, saw the colourful nymph
playing by a stream, and was so captivated by her that he
tried to persuade her off by
force. Her cries were heard by the rural powers who
changed her into a flower of many hues.

The Tulip was introduced to England at the end of
the sixteenth century. One legend tells how, when one
old lady introduced Tulips to her cottage garden, the
pixies were so delighted that they would sit with their

babies in them and sing them to rest. Often, at the beginning of night, a sweet lullaby accompanied by melodious music would float threw the garden on the air. The musicians were none other that the Tulips themselves, who would wave their heads in the evening breeze. As soon as the babies were lulled to sleep, the pixies would leave them while they went off to dance, returning at dawn to the Tulips, when they could be heard kissing and caressing their babies.

The old women would never allow a single Tulip to be plucked, so the happy pixies enchanted them so they would keep their blossoms longer than usual. When the old lady died, the pixies were heard singing sweet songs around her grave and no weed ever grew there, but the loveliest flowers sprang up without planting by mortal hand.

According to Hindustani legend, the Tulip, in a passion of jealousy, inspired by the exquisite lips of the heavenly fairy Bakawali, immersed itself in blood; hence the wound the tulip carries in its heart, the wound of unhappy love.

A popular ornamental for centuries, a huge industry is built around several thousand cultivars of the Tulip, especially in Holland, the country foremost in breeding Tulips.

Sister to the Star of Bethlehem and the Meadow Gagea, and beautiful in her many hues, the Tulip in her wild state favours the golden yellow brilliance of her true colour.

The Author

Marilyn Reid, (aged 51,) lives in the Highlands of Scotland, is a commissioned playwright, and has been a contributing editor on various topics for the Internet. Trained in Theatre Arts, Marilyn has been involved in the past in the tutoring, directing, writing for and setting up of many Community Arts Projects. Her main interests are History, World Culture, Folklore and Mythology, Scottish Culture and Belief (Studied at Aberdeen University.) Hill-walking, Writing, Reading.

Currently Marilyn is writing a new play entitled 'Silver Tides' for the Highland Year of Culture 2007. Marilyn's plays have previously been performed on the stage and local radio, and in schools around Tayside where she wrote under her previous name 'Cameron.' After many years working in theatre arts as a writer, director and tutor, Marilyn has produced a hand book for drama workers, teachers, and anyone else concerned with providing good workshops, entitled, How to Run Great Workshops and Set Up Your Own Theatre Group, ISBN 978-184753-386-9.

In recent years, Marilyn has concentrated on writing for new mediums such as the Internet, and local history publications. Two of her prior publications are currently on sale as information booklets 'The Broch Builders' (2002) and 'Glenelg Shadows' (2003.) Currently, Marilyn is researching for a new book about the famous Scottish bard 'RobertBurns,' and working on a long term project about a Scottish Botanist. Marilyn's website address is http://MarilynReid.com

Background to Mythical Flower Stories

When my adult daughter Hayley, suffered from a serious illness that left her disabled in the year 2000, she had to return home to begin the slow process of recovery. Whilst she and I took our slow walks together, we shared such pleasure from even the tiniest of flowers in both the gardens and in our beautiful surroundings in the West Coast of Scotland. After a long winter, I'll never forget the gladness we felt when the first snowdrops appeared in the Glenelg churchyard! That's when I decided to write these flower stories and the Snowdrop was the first of them. The first few were posted on my website at that time to gauge if other people would enjoy them, and then people began to e-mail me asking for information about their favourite flower. That's how this collection began.

My daughter and I have had many happy hours from them and every time we see a flower that we know a little about, or we are planting one, we smile when we recall its beautiful history. I hope you will have the same happy hours of discovery as we have. I hope you will also look at your flowers with a new eye, from reading these very precious flower stories. This book is dedicated to my daughter, whom, to me, is a symbol of bravery, dedication, and most of all, love.

If you have enjoyed Mythical Flower Stories, you will probably love Marilyn's latest publication Mythical Star Signs which you can find at Lulu.com